BREAKING THE RECORD

The Story of
THREE ARCTIC EXPEDITIONS

BY

M. DOUGLAS

Author of "Across Greenland's Ice-Fields,"

AUTHOR'S NOTE.

IT may seem presumptuous for an untravelled author to attempt to tell the story of the heroes who have bearded King Frost in his own peculiar realm; but should this modest chronicle of the adventures and sufferings of those kings of mighty men, who have successfully broken all previous records in Polar enterprise, tempt the reader to turn for fuller information to those true "human documents," Nares's "Voyage to the Polar Sea," Greely's "Three Years of Arctic Service," and Nansen's "Farthest North," in which what is here imperfectly narrated is set forth fully, my presumption may perhaps be forgiven.

M. D.

CONTENTS.

I.	A PROSPEROUS START,	9
II.	WINTER QUARTERS,	15
III.	SLEDGING IN ROBESON CHANNEL,	26
IV.	MARKHAM'S RECORD TRIP,	33
V.	WESTWARD HO!	47
VI.	IN GREENLAND,	53
VII.	HOMEWARD BOUND,	64
VIII.	THE AMERICAN STATION,	75
IX.	IN THE DARK,	82
X.	SPRING SLEDGING,	88
XI.	BREAKING THE ENGLISH RECORD,	97
XII.	GRINNELL LAND LAKES,	108
XIII.	GLACIERS AND ICE-FIELDS,	115
XIV.	RETREATING,	123
XV.	STARVING AT SABINE,	132
XVI.	FAITHFUL UNTO DEATH,	141
XVII.	DEAD YET SPEAKING,	153
XVIII.	FIRE AND ICE,	166
XIX.	STILL DRIFTING,	181
XX.	"A KING OF MIGHTY MEN,"	191
XXI.	FRANZ JOSEF LAND AND HOME,	208
XXII.	ON BOARD THE "FRAM,"	223

LIST OF ILLUSTRATIONS.

"FLOUNDERING THROUGH DEEP SNOW-DRIFTS,"	*Frontispiece*
COMMANDER MARKHAM,	19
THE "ALERT" IN WINTER QUARTERS,	22
"THE MOST NORTHERN POINT EVER REACHED BY MAN,"	40
BURIAL OF GEORGE PORTER,	44
THE "ALERT" NIPPED BY THE ICE OFF CAPE BEECHY,	68
THE "PROTEUS" CUTTING HER WAY THROUGH THE ICE,	78
DR. PAVY SETTING OUT FROM FORT CONGER,	93
RETURN OF LOCKWOOD TO FORT CONGER,	107
BREAKING UP OF THE ICE,	128
THE LAUNCH OF THE "FRAM,"	159
THE "FRAM" GETTING READY TO SAIL,	160
TROMSÖ,	162
WALRUS,	170
DOGS AND BEARS,	176
THE FIRST WHALE,	201
NANSEN ON HIS ARRIVAL AT ELMWOOD,	220

BREAKING THE RECORD.

CHAPTER I.

A PROSPEROUS START.

"ADMIRALTY, *May 25, 1875.*

"SIR, Her Majesty's Government having determined that an expedition of Arctic exploration and discovery should be undertaken, My Lords Commissioners of the Admiralty have been pleased to select you for the command of the said expedition, the scope and primary object of which should be to attain the highest northern latitude, and, if possible, to reach the North Pole, and from winter quarters to explore the adjacent coasts within the reach of travelling parties, the limits of ship navigation being confined within about the meridians of 20° and 90° west longitude."

So ran the first paragraph of the sailing orders issued by My Lords of the Admiralty to Captain

Nares, when, in command of Her Majesty's ships *Alert* and *Discovery*, he was commissioned to add one more to the already long list of attempts to reach the North Pole.

By the twenty-ninth of May all preparations were complete, and that afternoon the ships—duly provisioned for two years, and further supplied with all manner of gifts and comforts contributed privately by all sorts and conditions of men—cast off from their moorings in Portsmouth Harbour, and steamed down the Spithead amid the cheers and good wishes of thousands of spectators.

During the northward voyage the weather left much to be desired; but the Atlantic was crossed without mishap, and in the early days of July the ships were steaming peacefully along the west coast of Greenland, calling at Disco and other more northern settlements to take on board a few sledge-teams of Eskimo dogs, and also one or two Greenlanders who might probably be useful in various capacities. This occupied about a fortnight, and then, having left the last vestige of civilization astern, the explorers found themselves in Melville Bay, whose particularly aggressive ice has won a most evil reputation among Arctic voyagers. Unusually good luck, however, attended the *Alert* and *Discovery*. At first the ice was conspicuous by its absence, and when at last the pack was reached, they managed to pick their way through it without much difficulty, and reached Cape York

A PROSPEROUS START.

only seventy hours after leaving Upernavik, the most northern Danish settlement in Greenland.

This was a most satisfactory achievement, and all went pretty smoothly until the ships had passed through Smith Sound and reached Cape Sabine, where the real fight with the ice began. From this point almost every foot of the way had to be contested, and delays and dangers were of very frequent occurrence. Fortunately for the rate of advance, "night" had become merely a conventional term for a portion of the twenty-four hours, and for all practical purposes that period was indistinguishable from noon-day.

One evening, while pushing through a narrow channel which lay temptingly open, both ships very nearly came to grief; for before they had gone far the ice closed in around them. Escape was impossible, and the only thing to be done was to anchor to the biggest floe available; but as the pack pressed closer together, the pool in which the ships lay contracted more and more, and a severe nip became imminent; while, to make matters worse, the *Alert* was drifting down upon an iceberg a few hundred yards distant.

Nares signalled to the *Discovery*, "Take care of the iceberg;" and seeing the danger, Stephenson contrived to move his ship a short distance ahead. But the pack closed round her, and held her fast in a most perilous position.

The movements of ice are of a most casual description. In a few minutes the *Discovery* was in comparative safety, and the *Alert* was in greater jeopardy than before, as the floe to which she was anchored was every moment driven nearer and nearer to the berg, against which fragments of crushed ice were piling themselves in "most admired disorder." At last the crash came: the huge berg and the mighty floe collided with a force which, had the *Alert* been between them, must have crushed her like an egg-shell. Fortunately the nip just missed her; and when the sheltering floe broke up, it did so in such a manner that the ship, under the skilful handling of her crew, slid round the berg, and, with the *Discovery*, made fast in a small pool beyond it.

But the struggle had only begun. The ice was drifting rapidly southward; so, in order to make any way, it became necessary to ram the ships into the heaving, ever-shifting pack. For hours at a stretch the two captains never left the crow's nest at the mast-head, and it was only by their constant watchfulness that, more than once, one or other of the ships escaped a serious nip.

The *Discovery* seemed the better adapted for forcing a passage through the ice, so she generally led the way, steaming full speed at the opposing floes, and when necessary backing to strike a second blow. At each assault she cut through about twenty feet of ice, and it was found that floes of any thickness up to four feet yielded amiably to this treatment, but very hard or thick ice demanded a little more respect.

A PROSPEROUS START.

In his sailing orders Captain Nares was instructed that, " while both ships would share as far as possible in the objects of discovery and exploration, one must be so placed that she would not only serve for the crew of the other to fall back upon, but also that the united crews could escape from her to the relief-ship at the entrance of Smith Sound, by means of their sledges and boats, over the ice."

This second ship was on no account to be taken to the north of the eighty-second parallel; and when, on the twenty-fifth of August, the ships dropped anchor in a sheltered bay on the northern shore of Lady Franklin Sound, Nares saw that they had lighted on first-rate winter quarters. At first sight the snow-clad shores gave the harbour a very dreary appearance, and the crew of the *Discovery* received a good deal of sympathy in advance from their comrades on the *Alert*, but this quickly evaporated when a herd of musk-oxen was espied quietly feeding in the immediate neighbourhood. Several sportsmen set out in pursuit, and an elaborate scheme for the capture of the whole herd was evolved. The arrangements were beautiful, and it was only necessary for their complete success that the oxen should stay where they were. Unfortunately, this detail was beyond the control of the party; something frightened the animals, and they set off, full tilt, towards a deep ravine. But their flight availed them little, for as they neared the shelter two shots rang out, and a corresponding number of musk-oxen fell. The seven remaining cattle turned aside, but only to run into further danger; and in a short time the whole herd was laid low by the exulting hunters, whose morning sport resulted in the acquisition of over two thousand pounds of beef.

The rest of the day was spent by the two crews in an interchange of farewell visits; and in the course of the evening, Lieutenant Rawson and seven men from the *Discovery* took up their quarters on board the *Alert*. The plan was, that after the latter was settled in her winter quarters, the *Discovery's* men should return to their own ship. But "there's many a slip 'twixt the cup and the lip," and when, at the beginning of October, they essayed to return, they found the travelling in Robeson Channel so bad that after proceeding about twelve miles they were obliged to go back to the *Alert*. Not having expected to be absent from their ship for more than a few weeks, they had brought very few of their belongings with them, and in consequence, now that they had come to stay, they would have fared rather badly had not their friends on the *Alert* laid their own wardrobes under requisition. The ship's stores also contributed; and it was not long before, from one source or another, the eight "Discoverys" were as well supplied as any of the "Alerts" themselves.

CHAPTER II.

WINTER QUARTERS.

ON the twenty-sixth of August the *Alert* essayed to proceed on her solitary way towards the unexplored domain of eternal ice. She had successfully stormed the outworks of King Frost's citadel, but his icy hosts would not surrender their inner defences without a struggle. Before the *Alert* was clear of the harbour, the pack closed the channel; and when, after two days' strict blockade, the ice began to open, the tide was low, and an awkwardly-situated mud-bank held the *Alert* stationary. This was doubly annoying; but the rising tide speedily set her free, and as she triumphantly cleared the obstruction, she three times hoisted and dipped her colours. In reply to this valedictory salute, the *Discovery* ran up the signal, "Good luck," just in time to be seen before the *Alert* rounded the point which formed the boundary of the harbour.

Having at length succeeded in getting free, the *Alert* made her way without much difficulty to within a mile of Cape Beechy, where a large floe disputed the right of way with such effect that the rudder was rendered useless. The ice, moreover, was lying in heavy masses right up to the cape; so Nares anchored inshore of what were then supposed to be stranded icebergs, though, in the light of knowledge acquired later on, they were found to be merely sample floes of the real Polar make.

While the rudder was being shifted, five musk-oxen were seen on shore; and as meat when frozen would keep indefinitely, the sportsmen went in pursuit, and in a few hours sections of three of the animals were suspended in the rigging. The naturalist of the party, Captain Feilden, found also a wooden sledge and a stone lamp, which had evidently been left behind by some Eskimo hunting-party, as no trace of any habitation was to be seen. Probably game was not plentiful enough to tempt even Eskimos to wander further, for to the northward of this spot no trace of their presence was discovered. At length, from the vantage-ground at the top of the cape, the pack was seen to be opening, and an exciting race with the ice began. Would a huge floe which was drifting shorewards crush the ship against the cliff, or would she manage to escape? It was a close thing, but the ice lost the race, and about 10.30 p.m. the *Alert* anchored alongside of a big floe in Lincoln Bay. She might have gone a mile or two further, but the position chosen was the safest available should the pack close in, which it shortly afterwards did.

WINTER QUARTERS.

The heaviest ice hitherto encountered had ranged from twenty to fifty feet in thickness, but the Robeson Channel floes far exceeded even these very respectable dimensions. It was easy to credit them with an intimate acquaintance with the innermost recesses of the Polar Circle, for many of them were eighty feet thick, and from one to four miles in diameter. Such a thickness could not possibly have been attained in one season, and further observation of polar ice showed it to be of such evident antiquity, that the expanse of permanently frozen water to the northward of Robeson Channel was named by Captain Nares the Palæocrystic Sea.

Ice eighty feet thick was not a thing to be unwarily attacked, and the *Alert* was obliged to remain in Lincoln Bay until, on the first of September, the pack yielded to the persuasions of a strong southerly gale. Nothing could have better suited Captain Nares, for the wind also served to carry the vessel merrily on her course with a very slight expenditure of coal. Everybody's spirits rose. If only the wind would hold! But almost as soon as the wish was formed, the wind veered to the north-west, and shortly afterwards died away. The navigable channel became narrower and narrower, and just as the *Alert* cleared Robeson Channel, she was met by an impassable barrier of mighty floes which had closed in on the shore ice. Further progress was manifestly impossible, and seeing that the pack was bearing down towards him, Captain Nares took refuge behind some large grounded floes.

The weather had been misty, but a few hours after the *Alert* anchored, the fog lifted, and revealed a long line of coast stretching to the north-west and terminating in a bold promontory, which the explorers identified as Cape Joseph Henry.

A recent snowfall had covered land and sea with a shroud of dazzling whiteness; but, uninviting as the locality appeared, the explorers were fain to be content, for there was clearly no chance of advancing until those terrible floes ahead should move. This seemed to be about the last thing they had any intention of doing, and as time went on, instead of getting free, the *Alert* became more firmly walled in behind the line of "floebergs," as Captain Feilden designated the stranded monsters which protected the ship from the restless pack outside.

New ice now began to form rapidly, and the sun sank below the horizon at midnight. The short polar summer was at an end, and Nares plainly saw that the most he could hope to accomplish was to move the ship from her present exposed situation to some more sheltered harbour. But even this could not be managed, and when one or two attempts to better their position had signally failed, the explorers concluded to make the best of things as they were.

With a view to facilitating the work of the spring exploring parties, Captain Nares decided that before winter closed in sundry depôts of provisions should be established along the proposed routes. This was

COMMANDER MARKHAM. page 19.

WINTER QUARTERS.

far from being easy work, and one of the sledge-parties entrusted with it very nearly came to grief. A water-channel opened to the northward, and as this offered an opportunity of doing the work easily, Commander Markham, with Lieutenants Parr and Egerton and eighteen men, set out with boats and sledges over the two miles of rough ice which lay between the ship and the open water. They accomplished their mission; but as they were returning, a gale suddenly broke up the ice over which they were travelling, and it was only by great exertion that they contrived to reach the shore. There a new trouble awaited them; for the wind was in their faces, and they were almost blinded by a stinging drift of mingled snow and pebbles. Most of the men were more or less exhausted, and one poor fellow was so thoroughly done up that Markham put him on a sledge, and selecting the strongest of his comrades to drag him, sent him off to the ship. Then having found a sheltered camping-place for the others, he left Parr in charge, and easily outstripping the sledge, arrived late in the evening at the ship, or rather on the beach opposite to her.

Here also the gale had broken up the ice, and the wind was still so violent that Lieutenant Giffard and a strong boat's crew had enough to do to reach the shore; but they successfully accomplished the feat, and then added still further to their good offices by going in search of the sledge and its invalid occupant. The rest of the party came in on the following day, but several of the men were so much knocked up that they required the attention of the doctor.

About this time several of the dogs were attacked by an unknown disease. It was more like epilepsy than anything else, and between the fits the sufferers seemed to be unconscious of where they were and what they were doing. No Eskimo dog in his normal condition would venture on to thin ice, but under the influence of the fits the dogs lost all caution, and more than one was drowned by breaking through the ice. The doctors gave most kindly attention to the canine patients, and though they could discover neither cause nor cure for the disease, several of the dogs eventually recovered, but, unfortunately, a good many died. It frequently happened that while sledging dogs were attacked by fits; but, more often than not, if cast loose from their harness they came round, caught up the sledge, and were able to resume their work.

Before the sun took his departure for the winter, a good deal of sledging was accomplished. One or two parties went to Cape Joseph Henry, to find out how the coast lay beyond that point; but to their great annoyance no land was visible to the northward, and the pack-ice was so rough that it looked most unpromising for future sledging. But though this was disappointing, the sledgers had the satisfaction of feeling that they had placed one achievement to their

"FLOUNDERING THROUGH DEEP SNOW-DRIFTS." *Page 21.*

WINTER QUARTERS. 21

credit: they contrived to reach the highest latitude ever attained by man. Hitherto the palm had belonged to Sir Edward Parry, who in 1827 had reached 82° 45′ north latitude; but Markham's party improved upon this, and achieved the very respectable position of 82° 50′ north latitude.

This feat was performed at the cost of some trouble. Once or twice, in crossing new ice, the sledges broke through, more or less to the detriment of their loads, and the consequent discomfort of the party; but worse still was the terribly hard work of hauling heavy sledges through soft snow and over rough ice. The snow presented a most deceptively even surface: hummocks and hollows were alike invisible, and the men stumbled over the first or into the second as the case might be, varying their experiences by occasionally floundering through deep snow-drifts, or tumbling about on a sheet of new ice whose slippery surface was convenient for sledges, but awkward for men. This kind of work was, if possible, worse still for the dogs, who were altogether demoralized by the deep snow, in which they often sank to their muzzles. But they were willing fellows, and when it was reasonably possible for them to work, they did so most heartily.

The snow was bad enough when it was dry, but when it was wet and sloppy it was ten times worse; for it soaked through the men's foot-gear, and not unfrequently wet feet produced frost-bite. When the injury was discovered in time, no very serious effects ensued; but in some cases cold feet passed into a frozen condition without the sufferer finding out what had happened, and in consequence, when the sledges returned to the ship, May and several others had to submit to the amputation of one or more toes.

A minor inconvenience was the rapidly-decreasing daylight. The sun rose late and set early, and the sledgers being precluded from following his example, were forced, during the whole time that they were out, to breakfast and sup in the dark. Every day the departing sun gave them less of his presence: on the eleventh of October he set at one p.m., and on the thirteenth he made his last appearance for the season. From this time, although total darkness did not immediately set in, the amount and duration of light decreased daily, and on the seventh of November it was impossible to read a *Times* leading article in the open air at mid-day. The last few weeks of light were employed in banking up the ship with snow, housing in the upper deck, and removing all spare articles to the shore, where snow houses were constructed for their reception. The edifices received appropriate names, suggestive of the purposes for which they were employed—the storehouse being designated Deptford, the powder-magazine Woolwich, the observatory Greenwich, and so forth. The removal of all this gear considerably increased the available space between decks, and with the aid of plenty of

THE "ALERT" IN WINTER QUARTERS. *Page 22.*

stores and lamps, the *Alert* was converted into a very fairly comfortable Arctic abode.

During the winter the usual routine of shipboard life was completely altered, and since for all practical purposes the ship might be considered as a land residence, "shore-going" hours of working and sleeping were adopted. Each day brought its own occupations, and though the daily round of life and work may sometimes have seemed a little monotonous, everything went well. During the darkest period it was unsafe to venture far from the ship, but the doctor was so much impressed with the importance of fresh air, that he collected a number of empty meat-tins, with which he marked out a walk about half a mile in length. This promenade received the name of "The Ladies' Mile"—probably because it bore no resemblance whatever to the fashionable resort of that name in Hyde Park—and here, even on the darkest days, walking exercise was always practicable.

On the principle that "all work and no play makes Jack a dull boy," the evenings were always devoted to recreation. A night-school was established, lectures and dramatic entertainments were given, and a good many odds and ends of time were spent in games, dancing, and music: for the *Alert* possessed a capital piano, on which Lieutenant Aldrich was at all times ready to perform. Officers and men alike welcomed an excuse for a little jollity; even birthdays and Guy Fawkes's Day were duly observed, and Christmas was celebrated in true British style, with decorations, feasting, and fun unlimited. The jollification began on Christmas Eve with the distribution of cards and presents which the kindly forethought of friends, known and unknown, had provided in advance for every man on board. Altogether an exceedingly happy Christmas was spent; and at midnight on the thirty-first of December, when the ship's bell

"Rang out the old, rang in the new,"

the well-known strains of "Auld Lang Syne" echoed through the ship, healths were drunk, and the New Year opened on as happy and hopeful a set of men as could be found in Her Majesty's Navy.

On the seventeenth of January a faint crimson streak in the southern sky intimated that the long winter night was drawing to a close. Day by day the light increased, and by the first of February one or two sharp-eyed individuals contrived, though not very easily, to decipher a *Times* leading article out of doors at noon-day. Spring, though not yet come, was on the way, and the hares and lemmings acknowledged the fact by occasionally showing themselves. The latter were considered by Markham's dog Nellie as her lawful prey; she chased all she saw, and when she caught one, promptly devoured it, fur and all. This remarkable dog, though an English retriever, did not appear to mind the cold in the least; she delighted in a game in the snow, and would carry a stone or piece of ice in her mouth for any length of time. Had any of her human playfellows ventured to touch either object with the bare hand out of doors, he would probably have received a serious frost-bite for his trouble; but in Nellie's case no ill effects were apparent.

The return of daylight was the signal to commence preparations for sledging. This was work which called for the utmost care and forethought; for while it was most important that nothing should be forgotten, it was equally needful to avoid overloading the men, and everything—tents, tools, clothing, food, and medicine—had to be carefully weighed. It naturally followed that luxuries in general were conspicuous by their absence, but a moderate amount of tobacco was conceded; and the diet list included pemmican, bacon, biscuit, preserved potatoes, chocolate, tea, sugar, rum, lime-juice, pepper, salt, and a little curry powder to give a relish to the pemmican.

CHAPTER III.

SLEDGING IN ROBESON CHANNEL.

THE sledging programme was not arranged without much anxious thought. Captain Nares's orders ran—" If possible, reach the North Pole;" but this was a command which it was easier to issue than to obey. The ships were frozen in hard and fast; and even if the ice should release them, was there any chance that it would break up sufficiently to allow them to make much progress towards the Pole? Nares was decidedly of the opinion that nothing of the sort must be expected, and that the only hope of pushing northwards was by means of sledges; but then came the question—Was there any land to the northwards? and, if not, was the sea-ice traversable?

If such land existed, or if the ice to the north should prove to be stationary and traversable, it was on the cards that the following year a strong party from both ships might be able to force their way to the Pole itself. With this end in view it was decided, after much consideration, that a party led by Commander Markham and Lieutenant Parr should investigate the ice to the northward; that a second, commanded by Lieutenant Aldrich, should trace the coast beyond Cape Joseph Henry; and that a third, consisting of officers and men from the *Discovery*, should explore the north Greenland shore. Minor expeditions from both ships would meanwhile examine the fiords and hills in their respective localities. Thus a fairly extensive programme was mapped out, and the perils and honours of the expedition were equally divided between both crews.

It was necessary that Captain Stephenson should be made acquainted with the scheme, and the duty of communicating it was assigned to Lieutenant Egerton, who had been assiduously practising the art of dog-driving. He had arranged to start as soon as the sun reappeared above the horizon. But

"The best-laid schemes o' mice and men
Gang aft a-gley;"

and, owing to the extreme cold which set in about that time, it was not until the twelfth of March that Egerton, accompanied by Rawson, the Danish interpreter Neils Petersen, and a team of nine dogs, set out for Discovery Harbour.

At first all went well, but about lunch-time on the second day Petersen was seized with internal cramp. Some hot tea revived him a little, but the cold seemed to have taken thorough hold of the poor fellow; and though he struggled on through the afternoon, by the evening he was quite knocked up.

A second supply of hot tea and sal volatile had a stimulating effect, and his companions did their best to warm his chilled frame; but in the morning he was so weak and ill that they decided to give him a day's rest. This, however, was far from having the desired effect; for as the day wore on Petersen grew steadily worse, and the cutting wind, which found its way through every seam and opening of the tent, chilled him to the very bone. To warm him was impossible; but in the hope of making him a little more comfortable, Egerton and Rawson dug out a cave in a deep snowdrift, covered the entrance with the tent, and laid Petersen in the most sheltered corner. But even with the spirit-lamp alight the temperature only rose to 7°; and the two officers, with complete self-forgetfulness, wrapped the sick man in their own clothing, and, crouching beside him, endeavoured to thaw his feet against their bodies, although, as they afterwards said, his frozen limbs were so cold that, whenever they touched the skin, they scorched it as cold metal does in severe frost.

Night came at length, but it brought no rest to Petersen and his nurses. In the morning he was worse; and seeing no hope of amendment, Egerton and Rawson laid their patient on the sledge, and set out for the ship, which they hoped to reach before nightfall. Of course Petersen was well wrapped up; but no amount of clothing could keep the cold from him, and it frequently became necessary to stop, in order to restore circulation to his nose and hands. This caused a good deal of delay, but as the dogs knew they were homeward bound, they worked with a will, and even the frequent stoppages did not prevent good progress being made.

The roughness of the ice gave a great deal of trouble, and on two occasions the invalid was obliged to get off the sledge, and, with the aid of one of his companions, make his way over the obstruction on foot. During his second absence from the sledge, both it and the dogs disappeared into a deep chasm; and when they were extricated, the harness was in a woeful state of confusion. This necessitated a pause to disentangle it; but the dogs resented the delay. and bolted unceremoniously, upsetting both officers. Egerton retained his hold of the reins, but was powerless to stop the dogs, who continued their career until he became entangled between two pieces of ice, and thus brought his errant team to a standstill. He was not much the worse for his rough treatment, and the worst part of the journey being now accomplished, that same evening (the fifteenth of March), greatly to the surprise of their comrades, the sledge party arrived alongside the *Alert*.

Poor Petersen was in a pitiable condition; for in spite of all the care that had been bestowed upon him, his feet were so badly frost-bitten that it was necessary to amputate them, and parts of his nose and ears were in the same condition. For a time he seemed to mend; but the shock to his system had been too severe, and notwithstanding all the efforts made by the doctor to save him, he gradually sank, and died two months after his return to the ship. His comrades dug his grave on the brow of a hill, and marked his resting-place with a copper tablet bearing his name and the date, with the words, "He shall wash me, and I shall be as white as snow."

A few days after their return, Egerton and Rawson, nothing daunted by their misfortunes, again set out for the *Discovery*, accompanied this time by two sailors and seven dogs. For a few miles they got on pretty well, but after passing the spot where they had camped with Petersen, the steep snow slopes and abrupt declivities of the ice proved altogether too much for the dogs. It was frequently necessary to help them; but no sooner, with a "One, two, three—haul!" was the sledge dragged up one side of a hummock, than off rushed the dogs down the other side—a misdirection of energy which usually resulted in a general upset and entanglement. The road was about as bad as it could be, but one obstacle after another was overcome, and after several days spent in hauling, scrambling, and disentangling the harness when the dogs mixed it up, the travellers found themselves within a few miles of their goal.

Some little time before they sighted the ship, they came upon a path which evidently led to Discovery Bay. Even to the dogs the significance of this find was apparent: they pulled with renewed energy, and before long the last corner was rounded, and the travellers, tired as they were, saluted the *Discovery* with three hearty cheers which speedily brought the whole ship's company over the side to greet the new arrivals. For a time all was confusion: everybody talked and laughed and shook hands at the same time, while questions and answers tumbled over one another in a most bewildering manner.

When the commotion had a little subsided, Egerton and his companions learned that, with the exception of one man, all on board the *Discovery* were well, and that the winter had passed happily in a round of work and play similar to that which had occupied themselves. In one respect, indeed, the crew of the *Discovery* had had the advantage; for so many musk-oxen had been shot during the autumn that there had been no lack of fresh meat throughout the winter, though the beef in question was sometimes so strongly tainted with musk as to be almost uneatable. The reason of this was never satisfactorily ascertained, but apparently the taint was acquired when the animals were alive, and kept until some time after they were shot. Altogether the neighbourhood of Discovery Bay was considerably more interesting than the country near Floeberg Beach, and among other finds was a seam of excellent coal which cropped up above ground about four miles from the place where the ship lay.

Egerton's message was received with enthusiasm. Some of the *Discovery's* men had feared that little or none of the glory of the expedition would fall to their share, but Captain Nares's dispatches cut all ground from under this idea; and when Egerton and Rawson set out on their return journey, not only were preparations for sledging in full swing, but an advance party had already started for Greenland to investigate the condition of the provisions in the depôt at Thank God Harbour.

CHAPTER IV.

MARKHAM'S RECORD TRIP.

WHILE Egerton and Rawson were battling with the difficulties of Robeson Channel, their comrades on the *Alert* completed their preparations for travelling. Even the smallest details received careful attention; and, with the view of securing a little variation from the prevailing whiteness, the duck jumpers of the men had been painted with various bright-coloured designs, some of which showed great originality of conception on the part of the artists.

At length everything was ready, and on the third of April the sledges, gaily decorated with flags and laden with all manner of stores, left the *Alert*, and proceeded along the shore in the direction of Cape Joseph Henry, whence the northern and western parties would take their separate ways. To unaccustomed muscles the hauling was terribly heavy work, and nobody was very sorry when, after a short march as a beginning, a halt was called and the tents were pitched. While supper was preparing, sundry necessary duties were performed, and then the men pulled off their outdoor coats and foot-gear, put on dry clothing, and crawled into their sleeping-bags—an operation the reverse of pleasant, since, as a general rule, moccasins and blanket wrappers were frozen into a solid mass, while coats and coverlets had become as stiff as frost could make them. To wash while on the march was out of the question; for when, as was generally the case, it was a hard matter to get enough water to drink, no man, however devoted to cleanliness, was likely to waste any of the precious liquid on ablutions. In consequence of this deficiency, the faces of the explorers gradually acquired a depth and tone of colour which would not have been discreditable to a native African.

Supper—at which the principal dish was invariably pemmican—having been disposed of, grog was served out, pipes were lighted, and an hour or two passed pleasantly in rest and recreation; but after a hard day at the drag-ropes no one wanted to keep awake very long, and in due time the cooks ended their twenty-four hours' turn of duty by handing in the stiffly-frozen coverlets. Unless kept awake by the cold, all hands were soon asleep, and morning arrived all too soon for the new cooks, who began their duties an hour or two before anybody else was astir. As soon as the kettle boiled, a biscuit-bag was brought into each tent, cocoa was handed round, and while the pemmican was stewing, the men discussed their cocoa and biscuit, changed their clothes, rolled up the sleeping-bags, and otherwise prepared for the day's work. By the time all this was accomplished the pemmican was ready, the cocoa-bowls were filled with the steaming mixture, and as soon as they were emptied the tents were struck, the sledge loads readjusted, and another start was made.

At mid-day a halt was called, and the men kept themselves warm as best they could while tea was brewed. This took about an hour; but though waiting was horribly cold work, no one was disposed to relinquish the luxury of the tea, more especially as the bacon, which was always served out for lunch, was generally frozen so hard that until thawed in the tea it was quite uneatable. A slight soupy flavour was imparted to the drink by this process; but Arctic explorers cannot afford to be particular, and the bacon and tea were soon consumed. Then followed another spell of hauling, until the return of evening brought camping-time and rest.

Though April was only a week old, night, in the ordinary sense of the word, no longer existed, and the travellers had the benefit of constant daylight, which on sunny days sprinkled the snow with countless gems. The incessant glare was very trying to the eyes; but owing to the persevering use of goggles, only a few slight cases of snow-blindness occurred, and even Parr, who suffered more from this complaint than any one else, soon completely recovered.

Almost from the moment of leaving the ship the explorers' troubles began. Such a thing as smooth ice did not exist, and it took seven days to reach the depôt at Cape Joseph Henry. Here a general dispersion took place: two auxiliary sledges discharged their loads and returned to the ship; Aldrich, with his own sledge and an auxiliary, struck off to the west; and Markham and Parr with two sledges continued their northward route over ice which was almost impassable. Its condition called for extreme measures, and while Markham went ahead to select the best path, Parr and half a dozen men armed with pickaxes and shovels acted as navvies, and the rest of the party advanced the sledges, one at a time, as best they could. Occasionally a big level floe improved matters a little, but even then the snow was apt to be inconveniently deep, and day after day the roadmakers were kept hard at work. With all their labour, the so-called road could frequently only be traversed by means of standing-pulls, and the monotonous "One, two, three—haul!" which was the signal for each pull, became a cordially-detested sound. It was trying work, and after a few days a man named John Shirley complained one evening of pain in his knee and ankle. He had no recollection of having hurt himself, and as the joints were slightly swollen, Markham prescribed some simple remedy, which with a night's rest would, he hoped, set matters right.

MARKHAM'S RECORD TRIP.

Before morning the wind had risen to a gale, and clouds of drifting snow combined with intense cold made travelling a sheer impossibility. But about five in the afternoon of the second day, which was Easter Sunday, the weather having somewhat improved, the tents were struck. Poor Shirley, however, was no better. Possibly the cold had injured him, for he was now quite incapable of walking, and his comrades, having swathed him in wraps like a mummy, lashed him securely on one of the sledges.

Misfortunes seldom come singly: the following evening George Porter fell lame, and though with much pain and trouble he managed for a few hours to limp along, he was soon obliged to give up and submit to be dragged. The hauling strength of the party was thus greatly diminished, and as they had some days before reached the genuine palæocrystic ice, which apparently never broke up, Markham decided to abandon the larger of the two boats. This decision gave general satisfaction, for every one, invalids and all, wanted to push on as far as possible, and the absence of the big boat was a great relief, especially when, a day or two later, John Dawkins and Alfred Pearce had to be put on the sick-list.

Matters now began to look serious, for the invalids grew worse rather than better, and a terrible fear stole into the minds of Markham and Parr. What was this strange disease which was crippling one man after another? It was no mere lameness caused by overwork, for the patients speedily became powerless, and suffered from swollen joints, discoloured skin, faintness, and ever-increasing weakness. Could it be scurvy? Neither Markham nor Parr had ever seen the disease; but though they said nothing to the men, the fear in their own minds became greater every day. In each case the symptoms were the same, and several men who still were able to work complained of pain and stiffness in the legs, while early in May a fifth invalid, Reuben Francombe, was added to the list.

Day by day the travelling grew worse—or, as this seemed hardly possible, the increasing weakness of the men made it appear to do so. Even the weather was unpropitious, and on the fourth and fifth of May the fog was so thick and snow fell so heavily that the greater part of the time had to be spent in the tents. Markham consoled himself with the hope that rest and quiet would be good for the sick, but no effect was perceptible, and on the seventh of May the total distance made good after hours of work was only a quarter of a mile; for the same ground had to be traversed again and again, in order that the invalids, stores, and boat might all be advanced in turn.

Three days later Markham and Parr came, most unwillingly, to the conclusion that to attempt further advance would be madness. Not only were more than half the provisions consumed, but five men were entirely helpless, and the increasing stiffness and lameness of four others showed that before long they too would be disabled. To the officers it was clear that scurvy had broken out; but as yet the men did not suspect the nature of the ailment, which they called "Joseph Henry mange," and their leaders were careful not to alarm them. Nothing seemed to depress them; they joked each other about their lameness, and were still as anxious as ever to push on. Even the sick did not wish to turn back, though they had no comforts of any kind, and Markham had nothing to give them in the shape of medicine except a little lime-juice. Of this, two jars had been included in the stores, but both had been frozen solid; and on being put near the cooker to thaw, one fell to pieces. The other was saved from a like fate, and Markham hit on the plan of taking it into his sleeping-bag; but the success of the device was not great, for only a very small portion of the lime-juice consented to liquefy each night.

All things considered, prudence urged the wisdom of returning. But to be compelled to go back was a terrible disappointment; they had hoped to do so much, and in spite of all their labour and self-sacrifice they had accomplished so pitifully little. Having decided to go back, Markham thought it wise, before doing so, to give the men a rest; and he also wanted to take soundings and make a few other scientific investigations. With this end in view, he halted for a couple of days at the most northern camp: this was situated about four hundred miles from the Pole; but in order to ensure being within that distance, immediately after breakfast on the twelfth of May, all, except the invalids and the cooks, set out northward over villainous ice. They carried with them the sextant, the Union Jack, and some of the other flags.

At twelve o'clock they halted, the flags were unfurled, and as the sun for once shone out brightly, Markham was able to take an observation, which proclaimed the latitude to be $83° 20' 26''$ N.—exactly $399\frac{1}{2}$ miles from the Pole. In a few minutes snow began to fall; but heedless of the driving flakes, the men gathered round their flags and raised hearty cheers, first for the most northern point ever reached by man, and then for Captain Nares. The cheers were followed by "The Union Jack of Old England;" the "Palæocrystic Sledging Chorus," written by Mr. Pullen, the chaplain of the *Alert;* and last by "God Save the Queen."

The rest of the day was kept as a holiday, and a jovial evening was inaugurated with hare stew—the result of a lucky shot fired weeks before near Cape Joseph Henry. The festivities were crowned by some whisky toddy and cigars, both luxuries specially reserved for the occasion; and even the sick joined heartily in the songs with which the festivities concluded.

The following day the travellers, having deposited

"THE MOST NORTHERN POINT EVER REACHED BY MAN."

a record of their doings on a suitable hummock, turned their faces homewards. But the way was long, and with five helpless men to carry, in addition to the tents and other gear, travelling was terribly slow work; for the weights were too great for the waning strength of the men, and in order to make any progress at all, every inch of the way had to be traversed at least five times. Had it not been that they were retracing their steps over the road previously made, they could hardly have hoped to reach the ship; for if road-making had been added to their labours, it would have been impossible to cover the distance before the provisions were exhausted. Even as it was, had the men been able to eat their full rations, the stores would hardly have held out; but though little more than half the allowance of pemmican was cooked, even those who seemed strongest rarely managed to get through their portion, while the sick could scarcely eat at all. Constant thirst took the place of hunger; and this was a real torment, for, except at meal-times, there was nothing drinkable to be had. Fortunately the sun was daily becoming more powerful, and after a time the increasing warmth made it safe occasionally to suck an icicle, and thus obtain a little relief.

Very often the weather was thick and cloudy, but on clear days the dark rocks of Cape Joseph Henry could be seen looming clearer as the sledges slowly approached. On the seventeenth of May the travellers were still twenty-four miles or so from land, but that afternoon the tracks of a hare were seen clearly marked in the snow. The little creature seemed to have been travelling northward; probably it had lost its way, for the closeness of the footprints showed that it was almost exhausted, and had small chance of reaching land again.

Day after day the strength of the men declined, and by the end of May only seven were able to work. Progress became so slow and painful that Markham had to choose between abandoning the second boat, with the possibility that the ice might break up, and continuing to drag it, with the certainty that the provisions would be exhausted long before the party could reach the ship. One was a chance, the other a certainty; so of the two evils he chose the lesser, and decided to leave the boat and everything else that could be spared.

The day after the boat was abandoned a snow-bunting made its appearance. It was the first bird that had been seen for months, and even the sick roused themselves to watch it flying about.

On the second of June two more of the men were forced to give up work, and the weather became so thick and murky that the track made on the outward journey was finally lost amid a chaos of hummocks, where the pickaxe had again to be set to work. Had this occurred earlier, the consequences might have been serious; but the sledges had almost reached land, so, while the road-makers were at work, Markham and

MARKHAM'S RECORD TRIP. 43

Parr pushed on to the shore, where almost the first thing they saw was the recent track of a dog-sledge. Did this mean that help was near? It might be so, and with renewed courage they went on to the depôt, to the music of a condolatory welcome howled by an invisible wolf.

Near the depôt no sign of life was visible. If only they had arrived sooner! for on closer inspection they found that Captain Nares, with May and Feilden, had visited the spot, and had, indeed, left it only on the previous day. But it was no use to worry over what could not be altered; so taking three hares and some letters which the captain had left for them, the officers rejoined their men and camped for the night on a level floe about three hundred yards from land. The hares made a famous stew, and the next day (June 5) the worn-out men essayed to drag the sledges through the deep snow which lined the shore and rendered it all but impossible to advance. To reach the ship at this rate would take at least three weeks, and at the end of that time how many would be alive? Things looked very black, and as a last resource Parr—the only one strong enough for the task—volunteered to set out alone the next morning for the *Alert* and send help to his perishing friends.

Near Cape Joseph Henry, Flo, one of the Eskimo dogs, joined the party. She was seen first in the distance, looking wretchedly thin and miserable; but on being called she approached timidly, and gladly devoured some pemmican. Flo was a dog of distinct individuality of character. No matter how carefully she might be tied up at night, before morning she invariably contrived to free herself, and the men supposed she had escaped from the captain's team. However this might be, she now seemed very glad to have found friends, and tailed in with the cripples most amicably.

The next day the sun was shining brightly—so brightly indeed that though the temperature of the outer air was 30°, inside the tent the mercury rose to 82°. It was just the weather for Parr's long, lonely walk, and the belief that he would succeed gave his comrades new courage.

To one of the little band rest was very near. George Porter, who from the beginning of his illness had grown steadily weaker, was now in a most critical condition; but little or nothing could be done for him, and the day after Parr's departure he passed away. That same evening all who could walk followed him to his last resting-place, and while Markham read the burial service of the Church of England over him, the grimy, weather-beaten faces were wet with tears, of which no one even pretended to be ashamed.

A memorial stone was out of the question, but before leaving the spot the men placed over the grave a wooden cross with Porter's name, the date of his death, and the words, "Thy will be done."

BURIAL OF GEORGE PORTER. *Page 44.*

MARKHAM'S RECORD TRIP.

Meanwhile Parr was doggedly tramping towards the *Alert*. Tired and worn as he was, he was still in fairly good condition, and not until he had left twenty miles behind him did he stop. Then having reached a shooting tent left standing by some hunting-party, he made some tea, and having drunk it, resumed his tramp, until, on the second day, he reached his destination. No sooner was he on board than, without stopping to speak to the few men who were on deck, he made his way to the captain's cabin and told the whole sad story. Long before he had finished his tale the news of his return had spread through the ship, and even those who had heard no particulars understood that some terrible disaster had occurred. Grieved and shocked beyond expression, Nares lost no time in sending relief, and by midnight Lieutenant May and Dr. Moss, mounted on snow-shoes, were travelling northwards at express rate with a dog-sledge laden with necessaries; while a larger party, commanded by the captain himself, followed more slowly in their wake.

Never was relief more welcome. At first sight of the dog-sledge the colours were hoisted; but weak as the men were, the change from despair to hope was almost too much for them, and it was all they could do to raise a cheer as Moss and May came up.

That night even the sick managed to relish a supper of mutton, and the next day, when Nares arrived on the scene, Markham's anxieties were practically at an end. The presence of the doctor greatly encouraged the invalids, and, thanks to the willing help of the reinforcement, the remainder of the journey was quickly accomplished, and early in the morning of the fourteenth of June the returning sledgers arrived safely alongside the *Alert*.

CHAPTER V.

WESTWARD HO!

CAPTAIN NARES'S anxieties did not end with Markham's return, for Aldrich and his men were still out, and as they were already overdue, Nares became uneasy about them. Had they too fallen victims to scurvy? The captain thought it possible, and on the eighteenth of June he sent Lieutenant May with a dog-sledge and three men to search for them. A week passed without any sign, and then one day a newly-erected tent in the distance proclaimed to the anxious watchers on the *Alert* that the travellers were approaching, and a few hours later May came alongside with Aldrich and his companions in a condition which fully justified Nares's alarm.

At first all had gone well with them. The hauling, of course, was heavy work, and plenty of difficulties of the usual kind presented themselves, but they were far less serious than those which the northern party had to tackle, and fair progress was made. A discouraging feature of the journey was the persistence with which the coast ran towards the west: every headland that was passed revealed a further extension in the same direction, and when at length a change came, the shore turned abruptly southward. Not that it was always easy to decide which was land and which was sea, for, except at one place where a beautiful patch of green moss gladdened the eyes of the travellers, a white mantle of snow covered everything.

To make matters worse, an unaccountable stiffness attacked several of the men. For this the hard work in some degree accounted, and no one thought for a moment that an outbreak of scurvy had begun; the stiffness was supposed to be a mere passing inconvenience, which, on the principle that "like cures like," would in due time wear off. One of the first to be attacked was Sergeant Wood of the Marines, in whose case the disease took the form of an ugly-looking inflamed patch which, beginning on his ankle, in spite of a vigorous application of turpentine liniment gradually extended further, though for some time it caused him little inconvenience.

One evening when the explorers had been out some weeks, it was found that the pickaxe had been left behind at the last camp. To dispense with the tool was impossible, so Aldrich and Ayles went back the next morning to recover it. They could, of course, travel considerably faster than the sledge had done, and a few hours' hard walking brought them to the site of the last camp. But scarcely was the pickaxe secured when the rapidly-rising wind warned them to retrace their steps before the drifting snow obliterated the trail. There was no time for refreshment, and hungry and thirsty the two plodded on until they reached the spot where their comrades, who were making the best of their way onward with the sledge, had halted that morning for lunch. Here they paused for a morsel of food; but by this time the drifting snow had covered the track in many places, and as Ayles was beginning to feel symptoms of fatigue, whenever it disappeared from view he stood still; while Aldrich walked in a circle until he recovered the scent, and shouted to his comrade to come on. At length, being fairly tired out, they were thinking of spending the night in the snow, when the sight of the tent and the shouts of their companions told them that they had reached the camp, and in a little time the reunited explorers were enjoying the supper which the men's anxiety for the safety of the absent ones had hitherto prevented them from touching.

By this time it was obvious that there was no hope of reaching the North Pole by the west coast route, and as the men's lameness increased while the provisions rapidly diminished, Aldrich, a day or two after the pickaxe episode, decided to retreat. It was horribly disappointing to accomplish so little, but everything was against further progress; so the explorers hoisted the Union Jack at their most western point—85° 33′ west longitude—drank the Queen's health, and prepared to return.

The resolution was taken none too soon. Day by day the men grew weaker and less fit for work, while, to make matters worse, almost all disliked pemmican. No game had been seen for weeks, and even had biscuit been plentiful, as the disease increased the men became incapable of biting anything hard. At length they began to suspect that something more than mere hard work was causing their sufferings, and one day James Doidge asked Aldrich if "scurvy was ever got while sledging." Aldrich judiciously chose to regard the question as a merely theoretical inquiry, and on the strength of nothing of the sort having happened to previous expeditions, boldly answered "No," and proceeded to ascribe the sore mouth which probably suggested the inquiry to an undue indulgence in hard biscuit. The reply satisfied Doidge; but Aldrich, in spite of his cheery words, began to fear the worst, and his suspicions were confirmed when, in the course of a day or two, three men—Stubbs, Wood, and Mann—had to give up work.

The sun was now daily gaining power, and the softened snow greatly impeded the sledge; but difficulties notwithstanding, steady progress was made, and on the eleventh of June the explorers reached a depôt which had been established for them during their absence. An investigation of its contents revealed some very acceptable articles, among them lime-juice and preserved meat—the latter a most enjoyable change from the constant pemmican and the biscuit too hard to be eaten. Not less pleasant was a note which made known the good news of the well-being of the *Discovery*, and the men went on their way cheered and refreshed, though every day the sick travelled with greater difficulty and suffering.

It was manifest that to reach the ship without aid was impossible, and Ayles had already expressed his willingness to go on alone to fetch help, when Aldrich, who was reconnoitring a little way ahead of the sledge, suddenly heard a shout and the report of a gun. Looking up he saw Malley, one of the men who had accompanied Lieutenant May on the relief expedition dispatched by Captain Nares; and after giving notice of his presence by a wild shout, the lieutenant rushed back to the sledge with the good news. With friends at hand he gave up all thought of going further that day, and leaving Ayles and the others to pitch the tent, he went off in search of the party to which Malley doubtless belonged. He soon fell in with them, but his joy on learning their errand was damped by the sad news they had to tell, and fearing the effect of the tidings on the invalids, he asked the men not to tell them of the death of Porter and Petersen.

In their weakened state the sight of friends, and the knowledge that their trials were nearly at an end, almost overcame the worn-out explorers; but a good supper refreshed them, and in the morning they were quite ready to start again. With the help of the dog-sledge, which advanced the sick two at a time, progress became easier and quicker, and the unselfish fellows who rather than add to their comrades' loads hitherto had refused to allow themselves to be dragged if they could by any means walk, now showed the same consideration for the dogs, and essayed to limp for a while beside the sledge lest their four-footed friends should be over-fatigued. Everything now went prosperously, though some of the invalids were terribly weak ; and almost at the end of the journey Ayles developed a stiff knee—the result, as he said, of an injury, but, as Aldrich feared, of scurvy. However it might be, before the stiffness had time to develop into anything very serious the ship was reached, and rest and good food averted any further evil, though many weeks passed before some of the invalids received a clean bill of health from the doctor.

CHAPTER VI.

IN GREENLAND.

WHEN Egerton and Rawson reached the *Discovery* with Captain Nares's dispatches, the month of March was nearly ended; but so actively were preparations pushed forward, that by the sixth of April the North Greenland exploring party was ready to start, and Lieutenant Beaumont and Dr. Coppinger, with sixteen men and two sledges, set out for the *Alert*, whither Egerton and Rawson had already betaken themselves. As usual, the road was bad, and high winds delayed the travellers; but these were difficulties which perseverance could overcome, and in ten days they safely reached their destination. Four days' rest was allowed, and then the party, which now included Rawson and five extra men, began their march with four sledges, two of which were auxiliaries.

Knowing that the ice in Robeson Channel was very rough, Captain Nares had desired Egerton and Rawson, on their return from the *Discovery*, to pioneer a route for the main party. This errand had been duly discharged, and a road of some kind had been made; but near the Greenland coast the ice was so rough that half a day's hard work was necessary before the explorers could pass the shore-fringe of floebergs. From this point one of the auxiliary sledges was sent back to the *Alert*, and the rest of the party travelled along the shore, but at last the difficulties became so great that they betook themselves to the sea-ice. The floes were large and level, and as, judging by their thickness, they must have been several seasons old, Beaumont inferred that the tides and currents were less strong on the Greenland coast than on the west of Robeson Channel.

The snow was too deep to be convenient, and once more the explorers returned to land, but only to find themselves compelled to traverse a bank of hard snow which lay at so steep an angle that even to stand on it was almost impossible. Of course a road had to be cut, and Dr. Coppinger, who was in charge of the second auxiliary sledge, finding that the time at his disposal would not allow him to go further, here said good-bye to his friends. On his way back he visited a cairn erected by the Polaris Expedition on the north side of Newman Bay, and took from it the original record, leaving a copy with some notes of his own in its place. Sundry other articles were found, including a boat, some biscuits still in good condition in spite of four years' exposure to an Arctic climate, and more remarkable still, a chronometer, which on being wound up kept perfect time until the *Discovery* reached England.

It was unfortunate that Coppinger's return was not delayed a little longer, for already the first symptoms of scurvy had appeared in the usual form of swollen ankles. One or two men had begun to feel stiff before the doctor left, and James Hand, who had had several falls, spoke to Dr. Coppinger about his legs; but as the falls and the unusual exertion might very well account for the stiffness, the sufferer at first thought very little of it. Instead, however, of the lameness passing off, it continued to increase, and when after a few days several other men seemed knocked up, Beaumont halted for a day that they might have a rest. This gave him a good opportunity of examining the invalids, and though he had never before seen scurvy, the appearance of Hand's legs, and his description of his symptoms, tallied so exactly with what the lieutenant had read of the disease, that his suspicions were aroused, and he compared notes with Gray, one of the ice-quartermasters, who had often come in contact with scurvy on board whalers. According to Gray's experience, there was a likelihood of the disease passing off; but instead of mending, poor Hand grew steadily worse, and seeing that he was seriously ill, Beaumont requested Rawson to take the invalid to the depôt at Polaris Bay, and early on the morning of the eleventh of May the two sledges parted company.

For several days the northern party pursued their way through deep, soft snow, which made the hauling of a heavy sledge no easy or agreeable task. They crossed the mouths of several large fiords, which, had his party been larger, Beaumont would gladly have explored; but he could not divide his men, and his main object was to push northward as far as possible. That this would not be any great distance became distressingly clear, for the provisions were rapidly diminishing, and by the nineteenth of May almost half of the stock had been consumed. The sledgers were now struggling across an inlet where level ice was covered with deep snow, in which at every step they sank to their knees. It was almost impossible to move the sledge, but a few miles ahead lay a lofty peak called Mount Hooker, the summit of which promised a magnificent view of the coast line. This peak was now their goal, and sometimes, when the men could no longer walk, rather than stop altogether they crawled forward on all fours.

The dead level of the ice made it almost impossible to estimate distance, and for several days the land persistently appeared to be about a mile ahead. At last Beaumont could stand it no longer, and going ahead with Gray, in two hours they reached the foot of the cliffs. But Mount Hooker seemed nearly as far away as ever, and near the shore the snow concealed numerous cracks in the ice, many of them large enough to swallow up the sledge bodily.

For the outward journey only two days' provisions were available, and in that time no appreciable advance could be made. To drag the men on to the shore for no purpose would, in their disabled condition, be not only useless but cruel; and knowing that with all his determination he could do no more, Beaumont returned to the sledge, intending to halt for a couple of days before beginning the homeward journey.

Though Mount Hooker was out of the question, another lofty peak was visible considerably nearer, and this, Beaumont thought, might answer his purpose if the weather would but be propitious; but no! snow fell incessantly, and when the two days allowed for rest were over, the heavy flakes were still coming down with a beautiful persistency. But, snow or no snow, it was necessary to retreat, for by this time all the party, except Beaumont and Gray, were suffering more or less from scurvy, and two of the men were altogether disabled. It was fortunate that the old track was available, for travelling over it was so much easier than striking out a new path, that in two days the sledge covered a distance which before had occupied six days.

On the evening of the twenty-fourth of May the weather cleared, and Mount Hooker, now about sixteen miles distant, looked so tempting that Beaumont suggested that the two invalids should remain in camp while he, with the other men and a lightly-equipped sledge, made another attempt to reach the peak. The plan was hailed with delight; so the sledge was packed with some wraps and five days' rations, and all hands turned in for a few hours' sleep before starting. But again the disappointment common to "mice and men" asserted itself aggressively, for when the sleepers awoke the snow was falling as steadily as ever, and without a word the westward journey was resumed.

A few hours later the snow opportunely ceased just as the sledges reached a headland where Beaumont wished to build a cairn in which to deposit a record of his journey. This was successfully accomplished, and while the men rested, he and Gray ascended a neighbouring mountain about 3,700 feet in height, from which they obtained a magnificent view. Beaumont tried to make some sketches, but the cold interfered with artistic efforts; and when, after twelve hours' absence, the two men reached the camp, another snow-storm was in progress: in short, at this part of the journey the snow apparently left off falling only with the view of being continued shortly, like a serial story. Under such treatment by the weather the sick naturally grew worse, and by the third of June three men were unable to work, and two others, though still at the drag-ropes, only remained there by reason of a bull-dog pertinacity which would not allow them to give in.

Meanwhile matters had gone even worse with Rawson's party. Poor Hand did not improve at all, and two other men were attacked so severely that they soon became unable to work. This reduced the hauling force to Rawson and a marine named Rayner, while Hand became so helpless that he had to be placed on the sledge, where George Bryant ought to have joined him; but as he was just able to crawl along, the unselfish fellow steadfastly refused to lay any extra burden on his already sadly-overtasked companions. Long before Polaris Bay was reached, the provisions had come to such a low ebb that everybody had to be put on short commons; and to complete the misfortunes of the party, Rawson was so severely attacked by snow-blindness that for several days he was forced to travel blindfold. All this told against Hand's chance of recovery: he grew daily weaker, and a few hours after reaching Polaris Bay the poor fellow breathed his last. Bryant still continued very ill; but after a day or two Dr. Coppinger, who with Hans had been exploring Petermann Fiord, arrived on the seventh of June at the camp, and at once took charge of the invalids.

From that time affairs began to brighten, and thanks to Coppinger's skill and care, the sick were soon far on the road to recovery. This gave Rawson leisure to think of other things, and fearing that Beaumont's party might be in no better case than his own, he left Lieutenant Fulford in charge of the camp, and with Coppinger and Hans and a dog-sledge set out to meet Beaumont.

It was well that he did so, for fate was dealing hardly with the returning sledgers. Hitherto all had managed to walk, but one evening Charles Paul fell helpless on the snow. All power of locomotion had left him; and as he was unable even to stand, his companions, having wrapped him up as well as they could, laid him on the sledge. And a day or two afterwards William Jenkins was forced to give in. Two men were now helpless as babies, and their weight added to the already heavy load on the sledges was far more than their comrades could manage, and every foot of the way had to be traversed three times—first with the stores, then with the sick, and lastly with the tent. It was terribly hard work, and as Paul and Jenkins grew steadily worse, on reaching Repulse Harbour, at the mouth of Robeson Channel, Beaumont decided, instead of carrying out the original programme of returning by Polaris Bay, to make a dash for the *Alert*. Speed was the thing most to be desired, so everything that could possibly be spared was placed in a depôt at the harbour, and the little band turned their backs on the Greenland shore. But they were reckoning without their host. Since they last crossed the channel the sun and waves had been at work, and the travellers had scarcely advanced a mile when a large pool of black water, surrounded by rotten and untrustworthy ice, blocked the way. Beaumont was astounded; he had had no idea that the ice would break up so early in the summer, and though he could easily have gone round that pool, what might he not expect to find nearer to the western shore? Had his men been strong and active, they could doubtless have crossed safely; but as it was, Beaumont dared not risk the passage of the channel, and sadly enough the poor fellows turned their backs on the ship. Could they ever reach Polaris Bay, forty miles distant? The thing seemed impossible; but it was the one and only chance for life, and in spite of rapidly-failing strength and vanishing hope, they struggled bravely on towards the longed-for resting-place.

On the twenty-first of June the unlucky men met their crowning misfortune, in the shape of a heavy gale with violent snow-squalls which perpetually shifted their direction. No sooner was the tent pitched than down it went again; and as this occurred several times, the sick were placed on the sledge and covered as snugly as might be with the sail. This, however, proved a very ineffectual protection; for the drifting snow penetrated it in all directions, wetting the men to the skin.

To get warm was impossible, and when at last the march was resumed, everybody seemed to have suffered. Even Beaumont began to feel the stiffness and pain which generally ushered in an attack of scurvy, and the four men who were most ill gasped for breath if they attempted the smallest exertion. Two of them, Craig and Dobing, still manfully struggled on, but at intervals of ten yards or so they were forced to stop in order to regain their breath. At last they could hold out no longer, and were reluctantly obliged to take their places on the sledge. The daily advance did not now exceed a mile, for the working force was reduced to three, of whom Jones and Gray were so nearly worn out that when they broke camp on the evening of the twenty-fourth of June, Beaumont felt sure they had begun their last march. His intention was to encamp them all at the first suitable spot, and then make his way alone to Polaris Bay, where he hoped to meet some one from the ship.

But help was nearer than he had dared to hope; for while they were still wearily trudging on, he saw something dark moving along the shore. Hope dawned afresh at the sight, and as he continued to gaze, the unknown objects resolved themselves into Rawson's party, who thus opportunely arrived when help was most urgently needed. Dr. Coppinger at once took the invalids under his care, and finding that Paul and Jenkins were becoming rapidly weaker, he left the rest of the party in camp and pushed on with his two patients to the depôt. Unfortunately a rapid thaw had taken place, and as in some parts the ground was clear of snow, the sledge could not travel very fast, and the journey took much longer than Coppinger had expected. To all appearance, the invalids stood it fairly well, and on their arrival both were able to eat; but in Paul's case this was but the last flicker of the expiring flame of life, and in a few hours he had left earth and its sorrows behind.

Meanwhile Beaumont and his party, having advanced about three miles, found themselves compelled to halt and await the return of the dog-sledge, which after some delay made its appearance. Both dogs and men were very tired, but a good meal and a sleep refreshed them, and the same evening the travellers arrived without further adventures at the camp.

CHAPTER VII.

HOMEWARD BOUND.

DURING the absence of the three chief exploring parties the other members of the expedition had no cause to complain of lack of occupation. They had, indeed, too much rather than too little to do; for with returning summer a great deal of work became necessary, and in addition to this, sledges were employed for some time in taking out provisions for the use of the travellers. Sundry minor expeditions, also, were undertaken from both ships. Moreover, several cases of scurvy appeared, and a sledge-party commanded by Lieutenant Giffard, who was commissioned to establish a depôt for the western exploring expedition, suffered rather severely. Almost immediately after they left the *Alert* a man named Lorrimer fell lame, and grew worse and worse, until he became so bad that he could not walk. To take him forward or to send him back was equally difficult; so Giffard took the middle course, and constructed a snow hut, in which he left the invalid, with a comrade named Woolley to look after him. Woolley, though himself stiff and lame, was not too bad to satisfactorily discharge his duties as nurse and general utility man to the "hospital;" and when the sledge-party came back, they found that all had gone well during their absence. It was true that Lorrimer was no better, but, on the other hand, he was no worse; and when the journey was resumed, Woolley took his place as usual at the drag-rope. He became, however, more and more lame, and when the party reached the ship, he and Lorrimer had for some little time been keeping each other company on the sledge.

Early in May Captain Stephenson, with a large party from the *Discovery*, visited Captain Hall's grave at Polaris Bay, and erected a brass tablet to the memory of the American explorer. This duty performed, Stephenson and most of his companions returned to the *Discovery*, while Fulford and Dr. Coppinger, with two men and eight dogs, went to explore Petermann Fiord. The fiord was covered with heavy and apparently stationary ice, which, unlike most of its kind in the neighbourhood, was in some parts so slippery that even the dogs could not walk upon it, and several times the explorers were reduced to the humiliating necessity of advancing on all fours. The fiord contained several fine glaciers, and it was by no means unusual for a mighty avalanche to come tumbling over the cliffs. With so many obstacles to overcome, a thorough investigation of the locality was not feasible; but the fiord appeared to be the outlet of an immense glacier originating somewhere in the high ground to the eastward. From this exploration the travellers most opportunely returned, and met Rawson at Polaris Bay.

The outbreak of scurvy on board the *Alert* and among the sledgers caused much anxiety to Captain Nares. Well might he be worried, for with the exception of the officers, who for some reason had escaped the prevailing sickness, out of the ship's company only nine men were in good health. Certainly the sick were recovering, and would, in all probability, soon be quite well; but if one winter in the ice resulted in such an outbreak, what must be expected if a second were attempted? Moreover, could any advantage, scientific or otherwise, be gained by staying? It was obviously impossible to reach the Pole from any position which the ships could attain, and the most that could be done would be to explore a little more of the coast line. Was the game worth the candle? Nares thought not, and he decided to return to England as soon as the ice would permit.

Though the air seemed to have curiously little power of absorbing or radiating heat, the increasing power of the sun gradually took effect on the ice and snow. By the first of July every valley contained a stream, and the music of running water was to be heard on all sides, while the shade temperature rose to between 35° and 40°. Compared with the intense cold of winter, this very mild degree of heat seemed quite oppressive—so much so that fur clothing was discarded in favour of an informal attire of sleeved waistcoat, cricketing trousers, flannel cap, and knee or ankle boots. Before the month ended, on most of the hillsides the snow had given place to a carpet of grass and flowers. But the *Alert* was still hard and fast in the ice, without the slightest chance of making her escape until a strong south-west wind should cause the pack to break up. In view of this event everything was made ready for a start, and Parr undertook to clear a channel through the floebergs; but lest some wandering floe should enter and complicate matters, a slight barrier was left undisturbed until such time as the *Alert* should be in a position to apply the opening to its legitimate use. Patience was at length rewarded. On the thirty-first of July the long-desired south-west wind freed the *Alert*, and after eleven months' imprisonment she got up steam and emerged from her rampart of floebergs.

But her release was only temporary, for at the entrance of Robeson Channel the ice again brought her to a standstill. During the night the pack was constantly in motion, and in the morning a big floe was seen bearing down upon the *Alert*. It was touch and go, but fortunately steam was up, and she just managed to wriggle between the shore and the aggressive floe, which a few minutes afterwards swept over the spot so lately vacated. For a mile or two the vessel crept cautiously through a channel barely wide enough to allow her to pass, and after one or two more delays and narrow escapes of being crushed she reached Cape Union. Here she lay in security until the turn of the tide having changed the drift of the ice, and converted a position of safety into one of the greatest danger, Captain Nares took the bull by the horns, and forcing the *Alert* into the pack made her fast to a convenient floe. As the pack was in motion, the danger of this course was considerable; but, on the other hand, the ice was moving southward, and might be expected to carry the ship with it. Nares's confidence was not misplaced. In a little while the *Alert* was borne slowly and majestically past Cape Union and on down the channel, until, just as the tide was again about to turn, Nares seized a favourable opportunity of freeing the ship from the pack. Once clear he was fortunate enough to meet with no further obstruction until, near Cape Beechy at the southern entrance of Robeson Channel, the ice was found to be so firmly packed that until it opened progress was out of the question.

No communication had passed between the two ships since Nares had decided not to attempt a second winter in the ice. Captain Stephenson, therefore, knew nothing of the altered plans, and in order that no time might be lost in getting the *Discovery* ready for sea, Egerton once more undertook the office of messenger, and with one companion set out overland

THE "ALERT" NIPPED BY THE ICE OFF CAPE BEECHY. *Page 68.*

for Discovery Harbour. The distance was not great, but, unfortunately for themselves, the messengers lost their way, and wandered about over bogs and mountains for nineteen hours before they reached their destination.

The day after Egerton started, Rawson and two men arrived from the *Discovery*, and informed Captain Nares of the outbreak of scurvy among the North Greenland exploring party, who were still at Polaris Bay. Beaumont had, however, signified his intention of returning immediately, and might, said Rawson, even then be on the move. Under the circumstances a long visit was impossible, and after staying a couple of days on board the *Alert*, Rawson and his men began their return journey, during which, though they possessed no weapon more formidable than a big knife, a couple of musk-oxen lured them into one of the most exciting hunts of the season. Plenty of stones were available, and the sportsmen attempted by judicious pelting to drive the animals towards the *Discovery;* but this scheme was not agreeable to the musk-oxen, and placing themselves back to back, they prepared to meet the attack, whirling about on their hind legs in a most ingenious manner in order to keep their faces to the foe. The men, however, gradually closed in on them, and as their aim improved by practice, a few well-directed missiles struck the cow on the nose, so exasperating her that she dashed past her assailants and fled towards the hills. The calf being left alone, was now attacked more vigorously; but the plucky little beast having charged Rawson, who just managed to jump out of his way, followed his mother's example, and took flight. The men went in pursuit, and when the infuriated animals were once more surrounded, Rawson, finding that he could easily avoid their attacks, attempted to stab the cow with his hunting-knife. He wounded her two or three times, but could not kill her until, at the suggestion of one of the men, the knife was lashed to a walking-staff. The longer weapon was more successful, and another stab or two dispatched the unlucky cow.

Rawson then turned his attention to the young bull, who, puzzled by his mother's stillness, stood quietly watching her. The first stab, however, roused him to active defence, and he contrived to break away, and escape to the hills. Further pursuit was useless, and the men returned to the *Discovery* well pleased with their prowess.

Seeing no chance of relief, and having waited till his patience was exhausted, Nares at length resorted to force. A liberal expenditure of hard work and gunpowder had the desired effect, and on the twelfth of August the *Alert* triumphantly anchored alongside the *Discovery*. Beaumont had not yet arrived, and considering the disturbed state of the ice, Nares felt so uneasy that he prepared to go in search of him with the *Alert*. Lest a nip should occur while crossing the channel, all the invalids, official papers, and scientific specimens were sent on board the *Discovery*; but before this was accomplished the ice blocked the mouth of the harbour. In spite of his anxiety, Nares was powerless. It was impossible to get out until the pack moved; but while the *Alert* was awaiting its pleasure, Beaumont's camp was seen about two miles away, and Commander Markham with several men at once set out to meet the travellers.

The newly-returned sledgers had an exciting story to tell. They had left Polaris Bay on the evening of the eighth of August with one sledge, and a boat which, though the sledge was towed, was so heavily laden that she could neither be placed in the water nor transferred to the ice without being unloaded, and when afloat had only three inches of freeboard.

The first night good progress was made, partly in the boat and partly over the ice. The convalescents got on quite as well as could be expected; but Dr. Coppinger feared to overwork them, and after sixteen hours' labour the party camped on a large floe. Unfortunately the pack was in motion, and, to Beaumont's annoyance, he found, after a few hours, that the floe was being carried a good deal further to the south than he had any desire to go on such a raft. He at once aroused the men, but though they worked with all their might they made little progress, for the ice drifted southward as fast as they could travel northward, and at each halt more ground was lost. There seemed to be every chance that they would be swept on to Kennedy Channel, and once there, good-bye to all hope of reaching the ship. Should this happen, the lives of all would be in the greatest danger.

What was to be done? Land must somehow be reached, and even the convalescents forgot their weakness, and for thirty-five hours toiled unceasingly at the oars and drag-ropes. There was no time now to unload the boat in order to launch it—the chance of an upset had to go in with the rest—but no accident happened, and at length the travellers struck the shore of the tongue of land which formed the southern boundary of Lady Franklin Sound. Here there was no risk of further drifting, so, after resting for a time, Beaumont and Coppinger left the men to sleep, and went on by themselves to examine the ice in the sound. It seemed to be in good condition, and from the place where the officers stood they could see the two ships lying at anchor in the distance. Beaumont at once guessed that they were waiting for him; and considering it needless to make two bites of a cherry, for twenty-two hours the men pushed steadily forward. At the end of that time they were still some distance from the ship, and as a fog was coming on and the convalescents were tired out, they camped once more on the ice. In the morning the fog had lifted, and Markham and his men arrived on the scene before the camp breakfast was finished.

For a few days longer the ships were held in

durance vile; but on the twentieth of August the ice opened just enough to allow them to make their way out of Discovery Harbour, and in due time they passed through the pack which encumbered the mouth of the sound. Now for a time their troubles were over, and they steamed gaily down a wide waterway to the southern opening of Kennedy Channel. Here threatening weather made it prudent to take refuge in a land-locked and apparently safe bay; but, alas for the deceitfulness of ice! a passing floe drove the *Alert* ashore while the tide was running out, and before any steps could be taken to release her, the retreating water left her hard and fast aground. Fortunately she was in no way injured, and after a few hours, during which the insulted vessel lay at a most inconvenient angle, the rising tide again floated her, and what might have been a serious accident resolved itself into a temporary inconvenience.

New ice had already begun to form, and by the end of August it was strong enough to cause a good deal of trouble—in fact, the full force of the engines hardly sufficed to force a passage through it. The chief objection to this mode of progression lay in the lavish use of coal which it entailed, for as the supply was now reduced to a few tons, it behoved both captains to be as economical as possible.

Patience and perseverance, however, prevailed, and on the ninth of September the ships left the pack astern, and on the same evening reached Cape Isabella.

This was a notable event, for Commander Markham having landed "on spec," discovered a bundle of letters and papers which had been deposited shortly before by Sir Allen Young, the owner of the steam-yacht *Pandora*, which afterwards attained world-wide celebrity as the ill-fated *Jeannette*. Unfortunately, since Sir Allen's visit snow had fallen heavily, and a notice to the effect that the principal mail had been left on Littleton Island, off the Greenland coast, was effectually hidden. This untoward action on the part of the snow robbed the travellers of their letters, for they knew nothing of the neighbourhood of the mail-bags until they reached Disco. It was then too late to return, but a bundle of letters which had recently been brought by a Danish vessel partly made up for the disappointment.

Having obtained their letters, landed the two Greenlanders with the remaining Eskimo dogs, and procured a small supply of coal, the ships left Disco, and on the fourth of October crossed the Arctic Circle. Adverse winds made the voyage across the Atlantic longer and less pleasant than it might have been; but the explorers were in no mood to look on the dark side of anything, and when, on the second of November, they reached Portsmouth, a hearty welcome was accorded to the men by whose unselfish bravery new coast lines had been explored, and the British flag had been carried nearer to the Pole than ever mortal man had gone before.

CHAPTER VIII.

THE AMERICAN STATION.

ALTHOUGH the Nares Expedition had broken all previous records and explored many miles of hitherto unknown coast line, much still remained to be done. The Pole, for all practical purposes, was as far off as ever; an unknown extent of coast line was still untraversed; the interior of Greenland and Grinnell Land had never been visited; while knowledge of the magnetic, meteorological, and other scientific conditions of the Arctic regions was at an extremely low ebb. This condition of affairs was, naturally, unsatisfactory to the scientific world, and at a congress which met at Rome in April 1879 it was agreed that, in accordance with a suggestion made some years before by Lieutenant Weyprecht, the discoverer of Franz Josef Land, at various points in the Polar regions observation stations should be established.

Several nations took part in the work, among them the United States of America, where the project excited the liveliest interest. It was arranged that Discovery Bay should be adopted as the American station, and arrangements were made under the auspices of the War Department, though on such a service only men who volunteered for the work were employed. Many of these, both officers and men, being members of the signal corps, had received special scientific training; but others were from the ordinary rank and file, and a few were specially enlisted for the expedition, the command of which was entrusted to Lieutenant Adolphus W. Greely. The other officers were Lieutenant Frederick F. Kislingbury, Lieutenant James B. Lockwood, and Surgeon Octave Pavy.

Though the expedition was more or less under consideration for some time, the final arrangements were hurriedly made. The experience of other expeditions, however, left no vagueness as to the provisions, clothing, and equipment necessary; and though a little more time might well have been bestowed on the preparations, taking everything into consideration they were fairly complete, and on July 7, 1881, the *Proteus*, with men and stores on board, set sail from St. John's, Newfoundland.

At first thick weather caused some delay, and in less than a week the ship encountered ice off the Greenland coast; but the pack was not disposed to be aggressive, and a couple of days later the explorers found themselves at Godhavn, where the Danish officials accorded them the heartiest of welcomes. Here Dr. Pavy joined the expedition, which was

THE AMERICAN STATION.

further augmented by the acquisition of twelve dogs. These considering themselves by right of priority of arrival the canine possessors of the ship, felt aggrieved by the subsequent appearance of two more teams embarked at Ritenbenk and Upernavik, and a war ensued which no amount of battles could decide. As dog-driving is an art not usually practised in the United States, two Eskimos were engaged at Upernavik, and then, arrangements being complete, the *Proteus* again got up steam.

A day or two later the first bear was seen. He was calmly devouring a seal; and taking advantage of his preoccupation, the sportsmen opened fire. Bruin was too confiding or too lazy to run away, and a boat having been lowered he was easily secured; though, as the honour of firing the fatal shot was claimed by three or four different men, no one was able to decide who was really the successful marksman.

Melville Bay was unusually clear of ice, and the ship made her way without difficulty to Littleton Island, where the undiscovered mail left behind by the Nares Expedition was hunted up and recovered. Some coal was landed to form a depôt; but as the sea to the northward was open, it was considered unwise to delay long, and the expedition went on its way, rejoicing at the success which so far had attended it. Stopping occasionally with a view to examining or forming depôts, the explorers proceeded, without opposition from the ice. to the mouth of Lady

Franklin Bay. Here a wall of ice barred further progress. It was aggravating to be stopped so near their destination, but patience was the only remedy for the evil. For several days no advance was practicable, and under the malign influence of a north-easterly gale the *Proteus* was driven at least forty miles to the southward. But nothing lasts for ever, and in course of time the wind changed and opened the pack. All obstacles were now removed, and on the eleventh of August the vessel anchored in Discovery Bay, though the ice would not at first allow her to approach the shore.

History, it is said, repeats itself, and, as on the occasion of the arrival of the British ships in 1875, the first thing seen was a musk-ox. Naturally a party at once started in pursuit, and before long that musk-ox was secured. This was the first of many musk-oxen slain during the sojourn of the expedition in Discovery Bay. The animals were fairly plentiful, and the hunters generally managed to keep the larder supplied.

Near the shore the ice varied from sixteen inches to ten feet in thickness; but the iron prow of the *Proteus* and the ingenuity of her captain together overcame this difficulty, and by dint of alternately backing and charging the ice, she cut her way through it, and finally anchored within a hundred yards of the beach.

Hitherto the explorers had merely been passengers,

THE "PROTEUS" CUTTING HER WAY THROUGH THE ICE. *Page 78.*

THE AMERICAN STATION.   79

but now their work began. A site for the house was chosen, and the carpenters set to work to build, while all the others, except three or four who were necessarily otherwise engaged, assisted in unloading and landing the stores, timber for the house, and other paraphernalia. The work progressed so fast that in a week everything was landed, and the ship was free, as soon as the ice would permit, to begin her homeward voyage, taking with her a couple of men who were physically unfit for Arctic service. About this time Lieutenant Kislingbury became dissatisfied, and requested to be relieved from duty. This was done, and he too would have gone home, but the *Proteus* sailed before he had time to get on board. He was forced, therefore, to remain with the expedition, though he took no share in the work except as a volunteer.

Meanwhile building operations made rapid progress, and in a few days Fort Conger (so named in honour of Senator Conger, who had done much to promote the dispatch of the expedition) was in a fair way to completion. Some of the party moved in as soon as the roof was on, but the others elected to remain under canvas until the house was more complete. The edifice measured sixty feet in length, and seventeen in width inside the walls, which were constructed of wood well covered with tarred paper to keep out draughts.

The centre of the domicile was occupied by a small entrance-hall, on one side of which was a large apartment which served as living and sleeping room for the men, and on the other a similar but smaller room for the officers. A miniature kitchen occupied as much of the central space as was not required for the entrance-hall, and between the roof and the board ceiling a variety of articles were stored, while others were bestowed in lean-to erections at each end of the main building. Another "modern convenience" supplied to this desirable Arctic residence was a well-warmed bath-room.

During the winter the outer walls were banked with snow, which excluded draughts; and when curtains had been arranged around the bunks, and each man had disposed his various possessions on shelves above his bed, the mansion really became quite comfortable.

The surrounding country was mountainous, and did not look very promising for sledging. This, however, was one of the main objects of the expedition, and soon after the house was finished sundry short trips were undertaken with the view of inspecting existing depôts, establishing new ones, and studying the lie of the land. But short though the trips were, they gave the men a good insight into the disagreeables of Arctic travelling; for by the end of August sharp frosts set in, and one or two frost-bites, as well as a sharp attack of rheumatism which for a few days crippled Sergeant Rice, resulted from wet feet. Sometimes actual danger was added to the many discomforts of the work, and one night Dr. Pavy, Private Whisler, and one of the Eskimos were obliged to camp on a narrow ice-foot. This itself was insecure, and to add to the drawbacks of the position, on one side of the camp was a high cliff down which stones were perpetually rolling, and on the other sundry stranded floebergs threatened, under pressure from a heavy gale, to overturn at any moment.

During the autumn Lieutenant Kislingbury and one or two others put in a good deal of time in hunting. So marked was their success that before the sun departed six musk-oxen, ten ducks, one hare, one ptarmigan, and two seals had been added to the larder. Wolves, too, were seen, and several were shot; but, like many other Arctic animals, they were wonderfully tenacious of life, and even when very severely wounded, sometimes contrived to escape.

The presence of the wolves considerably alarmed the dogs, and as Greely feared some of the latter might fall victims to the hungry prowlers, he decided to lay down some poison. But it is one thing to lay down poison and another thing to induce wolves to pick it up, and when poisoned meat was put down by itself, the wolves, probably disliking the smell, carefully refrained from touching the deleterious morsels. Even when poisoned and unpoisoned meat were mixed together, they sometimes contrived to eat the good and avoid the bad. Finally four of them were killed, and then the rest of the pack took their departure.

CHAPTER IX.

IN THE DARK.

DURING the northward voyage the scientists of the expedition, eager to begin work, had improved the time by taking frequent observations of the temperature of the water both on the surface and at various depths. With such ardent seekers after knowledge, little time was likely to be wasted, and even the bustle of landing, house-building, and settling into their quarters did not suffice to turn them from the even tenor of their way, and they continued to make observations and notes on the atmosphere, the temperature, the clouds, the weather, the auroras, the wind, the magnetic conditions, and on everything else which could be observed and noted. They were determined to add something to the sum of the world's knowledge by their sojourn in the far North, and in so far as they could do this they would reap the reward of their labours.

To this part of the work the absence of the sun made little difference, and all through the winter the observations were continued without intermission, in

IN THE DARK.

spite of the discomfort of such pursuits when the thermometer indicated sixty degrees or so of frost. With other work—sledging, hunting, and outdoor occupations in general—the case was different. These could not be pursued in the dark; but as a lengthy period of inaction was likely to be injurious, both physically and morally, Greely put off its commencement as long as possible, and for some time after the disappearance of the sun short sledging excursions were undertaken. Some of the men were set to work as colliers, and a good deal of coal was dug from the seam discovered by the Nares Expedition. This contributed much to the comfort of the sledgers; for both at Cape Murchison and Cape Beechy a snow-house was built and a stock of coal accumulated for the benefit of future sledging-parties.

Long before winter set in life at Fort Conger had settled down into a routine which, except in matters of detail, varied little from day to day. Sunday was always kept as a holiday, and though the party included men of various religious beliefs, the reading of the Psalms for the day was a form of divine service in which all could join. The rest of the day, when the light permitted, was generally spent in hunting, strolling about, or any other occupation that commended itself to individual tastes, though Greely announced that he expected all games to be eschewed.

A fairly extensive selection of tinned provisions

had been provided, so with the addition of the game obtained on the spot the diet list was sufficiently varied. The bill of fare included fresh meat, tinned meats, soups, fish, vegetables and fruits, cheese, oatmeal, butter, preserved milk, peas and beans, hard bread and fresh-baked bread. Breakfast was served at 7.30 a.m., and dinner at 4 p.m., and at mid-day and in the evening a lunch, as the men called it, of hard bread, butter, tea, and coffee, was put on the table for everybody to help himself as he chose.

As the expedition did not boast a professed cook, the men took it in turn to preside in the kitchen— a plan which, if it did not ensure good cooking, at any rate prevented a monotony of method. Fortunately nobody was very particular, though several of the men had a strong aversion to tea.

Towards the middle of December, in spite of as much variety of work and amusement, both outdoor and indoor, as could be arranged, some of the party began to suffer from the long-continued darkness. On some minds it had a very depressing effect, and strangely enough the Eskimos seemed more affected than the Americans. One of them named Jens Edward nearly went out of his mind: in a fit of aberration he wandered off breakfastless, and it was some time before the search-party which was at once sent out succeeded in finding him and bringing him back. They did not accomplish this errand entirely without disaster, for Sergeant Rice found it impossible to keep his feet in scrambling over the rough ice: after sundry falls he severely injured his shoulder, and was sent back to Conger under the care of Private Whisler. Long before they reached the station, however, nurse and patient had changed places; for Whisler had neglected to put on sufficient clothing, and the effect of the cold was to throw his mind temporarily off its balance. It also deprived him of all strength, and Rice had the greatest difficulty in conveying his quondam nurse to Conger.

Twice during the winter an unpleasant excitement occurred in the form of a fire in the carpenter's shop. The first time several tools were destroyed, and at the second conflagration Sergeant Elison, who had caused the disaster by injudiciously attempting to fill a gasoline lamp while it was alight, paid for his folly by the loss of his beard, eyebrows, and part of his hair, not to mention several severe burns on face and hands. Sixty-four degrees of frost made the work of extinction both difficult and disagreeable; but the amateur fire-brigade went gallantly to work, succeeding so well that very little damage was done, except to the sergeant's personal appearance.

As time went on the canine portion of the expedition was reinforced by the arrival of numerous puppies. The mothers were sometimes afflicted with cannibal tendencies, and on occasion would devour each other's puppies; so it was found necessary to appoint a responsible person to act as head-nurse.

This arduous office was accepted by Private Schneider, who fulfilled its duties so efficiently that fifteen of the pups passed safely through the various stages of puppyhood, and reached dog's estate. They soon became hardy little fellows, full of fun and mischief, and quite indifferent to cold. One night, with something like seventy degrees of frost, several of them rushed out of doors to inspect some water which had been thrown out. It contained a few scraps of eatables, and while busy nosing out these, two or three puppies were frozen to the ground so firmly that they could not release themselves, and some one had to go to their assistance with a hatchet.

Christmas was, as usual, a festive season. To begin with, the house was thoroughly cleaned and scrubbed, though whenever water touched the floors it promptly froze into a coating of ice which had to be scraped off. Decorations were put up, and by Christmas Eve the establishment presented an altogether festive appearance; and when Greely brought out sundry boxes containing presents from home, a merrier party it would have been difficult to find. Next day the feasting began: all sorts of delicacies were produced from the stores, and in spite of Arctic frosts the ice-creams, so dear to Americans, figured conspicuously on the menu.

Christmas Day that year fell on Sunday, so theatrical and other amusements were postponed until Boxing Day, when the men gave a very good variety entertainment which included a most realistic Indian representation. The arrival of the New Year was another occasion for jollity, and the light of the full moon encouraged the men to attempt outdoor sports, in addition to dancing the old year out and the new year in.

The sixteenth of January was marked by a terrible storm and gale, which for some hours rendered it quite impossible to venture outside the door. Greely expected every moment to see the roof carried away; but, rather to his surprise, it held firm, though the anemometer was broken by the violence of the gusts. Just before this happened the gale had attained a velocity of sixty-five miles an hour, and it was, doubtless, only the snow-banks which had been raised around the house that saved the edifice from destruction.

CHAPTER X.

SPRING SLEDGING.

THOUGH the sun did not reappear until the end of February, at the beginning of that month darkness began to give place to light, and on the 2nd the thermometer outside the house was read without the aid of artificial light. The cold seemed to increase rather than diminish with the return of daylight, for that same day the spirit thermometer indicated a temperature of $-64.8°$. Extremely cold weather continued for some days, and a variety of experiments was made with the view of ascertaining what degree of cold was required to freeze various liquids, such as alcohol, chloroform, brandy, spirits of turpentine, and nitric acid.

With a temperature of $-55°$, less than an hour's exposure converted the brandy into solid ice, and caused the nitric acid to assume the consistency of lard. The turpentine showed no signs of solidifying until the thermometer fell to $-59.4°$, and at the same temperature chloroform was so far affected that small spikelets formed near the bottom of the vessel; the alcohol remained apparently unaltered.

Such a degree of cold might very well have been expected to affect the dogs; but throughout the winter the only thing they seemed to mind was the wind. This, combined with the frost, was too much even for them, and, much as they generally disliked to sleep under cover, sometimes forced them to seek shelter in a tent which was erected for their benefit. Though indifferent to cold, they did not object to warmth, and the ash-barrel, the contents of which presumably contained some degree of heat, was a much-coveted resting-place. Unfortunately it was only large enough to accommodate one dog at a time, and was, in consequence, a fruitful source of dissension and disappointment to unsuccessful competitors for the eligible position.

The return of daylight set the hunters once more to work, and on the fifteenth of February Jens shot the first hare of the season. The animal had a magnificent coat of white fur, and had evidently managed to fare well during the winter; for it was in splendid condition, and weighed eleven pounds before it was skinned. The next day two more hares were shot; but as yet the stock of fresh meat accumulated in the autumn was far from being exhausted, and there was no reason to fear that the supply would run short for some time to come.

Meanwhile active preparations for sledging were

in progress. Every detail, not only of provisions and stores, but also of the construction of the sledges, received most careful attention. Profiting by the experience of the Nares Expedition, Greely somewhat increased the allowance of food, and instead of supplying nothing in the meat line but pemmican and bacon, he added to the sledging rations frozen musk-meat, tinned sausage, and corned beef. Lime-juice had, unfortunately, been mixed with the pemmican; but however valuable this may have been theoretically, practically it was extremely unpopular.

Even in the coldest winter weather few of the party had cared to wear furs, and now, with sledging in prospect, they still preferred to stick to heavy woollen clothing. This was contrary to the usual practice of Arctic travellers, but the innovation was, on the whole, an improvement, and nobody found cause at any time to regret it. For foot-gear the moccasin or the Greenland boot was used, and the travelling attire of the sledgers was completed by woollen mittens and leather caps lined with flannel or cloth. Altogether the "rig-out" was warm and comfortable, and proved entirely suitable to the occasion.

The first expedition of the season was undertaken by Lieutenant Lockwood, Sergeant Brainard, and Eskimo Christiansen. Their mission was simply to reconnoitre, and having successfully performed their errand, they returned to the fort before the sun made his appearance above the horizon. He had, in fact, barely accomplished this feat when the same party, augmented by the presence of Sergeant Jewell, was again afoot, this time to inspect the depôts and report on the state of the ice on the Greenland shore. On this occasion the floes on Robeson Channel were in fairly good condition, and though in places the snow was deeper than might have been desired, the dogs made good progress, and a few hours after the party left the depôt at Cape Beechy they camped on Greenland soil. Travelling southward, they soon reached Thank God Harbour, where they spent a day in overhauling the contents of the depôt. A good many eatables and a number of other articles were found to be in good condition, and two coverlets which Lieutenant Beaumont had left behind when he broke up his camp were joyfully annexed, as the thermometer that evening indicated the cheerful temperature of $-51°$, and any amount of wraps were, in consequence, acceptable.

Having visited the graves of Captain Hall and the two English sailors Paul and Hand, Lockwood and his companions set out overland for Newman Bay. The ground was remarkably free from snow, but extreme cold continued, and after six hours' work, as a storm threatened, the party decided to halt. A hut was constructed in a convenient snow-drift— none too soon; for scarcely were the travellers ensconced within than the wind rose and snow began to fall heavily, though the thermometer still stood at $-50°$. In the open air this would have been unendurable, but inside the shelter the temperature rose considerably, and owing to deficiency of ventilation the inmates were nearly stifled; even the entrance was blocked by the drifting snow, and when the storm subsided they had to dig themselves out of their prison.

Unfortunately the subsidence of the storm was only temporary, and the cold wind caused so many minor frost-bites that Lockwood again halted. Another snow residence was constructed, and this, like its predecessor, was peculiarly air-tight—so much so that when the men attempted to light their cooking-stove, the matches could not be induced to burn in the vitiated atmosphere. To make matters worse, the supply of matches had run short, and as one after another was struck only to flicker out immediately, things began to look serious, and the unpleasant prospect of having to endeavour to reach Fort Conger without means of procuring water forcibly presented itself. Finally, after many attempts, a piece of paper was induced to ignite; with this the lamp was lighted, and profiting by their experience, the sledgers did not allow it to go out again while they remained in camp. In consequence, the temperature inside the hut rose considerably; but this, though in some ways pleasant, was not without its attendant disadvantages: for the sleeping-bag absorbed so much moisture that

DR. PAVY SETTING OUT FROM FORT CONGER.   *Page 93.*

SPRING SLEDGING.

when exposed to the air it froze as hard as iron, and at the next camping-place the whole strength of the four men was required to unroll it. But in spite of hardships the expedition was a distinct success; the party learned all they desired to know, and seeing that everything promised well for future operations, they returned in good spirits to Conger.

A great part of March was spent in establishing depôts, chiefly on the Greenland coast; but about the middle of the month Dr. Pavy, Sergeant Rice, and Jens, with a first-rate dog team, departed northwards, hoping to pass Commander Markham's furthest point, and also to discover land which might form a suitable base for a sledge journey, if luck would have it so, to the Pole itself.

As usual in Robeson Channel, travelling was anything but easy. The shore ice in places was untraversable, and when in despair the sledge was lowered by means of its traces to the floe, matters were not much better. It was clear that the channel was not designed by nature for sledging purposes, and at one place sledge and load had to be carried for a hundred yards or so. The rough treatment which the runners received soon proved too much for them, and before Cape Union was reached one of them split from end to end.

No spare runners had been brought, so, as the sledge could not travel further in its crippled condition, Rice and Jens returned to Conger. Carrying nothing except a small spirit-lamp, a little meat and chocolate, and the steel shoe of the damaged runner, they were able to travel rapidly, and in one march reached Cape Beechy. Jens was almost knocked up by the exertion, but after a few hours' rest he was able to go on; and having procured the necessary runner, the two men in due time rejoined Pavy, who, with the dogs, was awaiting them at Lincoln Bay.

Passing the stone which marked the resting-place of Neils Petersen, the Danish interpreter of the *Alert*, Pavy and his companions pursued their way towards Cape Joseph Henry. Greely had suggested that the journey should begin from James Ross Bay on the west of the cape; but finding the land travelling bad, Pavy decided to take Markham's route, and instead of crossing Feilden Peninsula, to keep to the east of Cape Joseph Henry. Here the ice was new and good, and for a time all went merrily; but no sooner were the explorers on the palæocrystic floes of Lincoln Sea, than a very different scene presented itself. Here, there, and everywhere hummocks large and small, piled up in "confusion worse confounded," blocked the way, just as they had done on the occasion of Markham's journey. In one direction only—north-westward—did there seem to be any chance of advancing. There the ice was smoother, and the travellers pushed forward with rising hopes of being able to accomplish something memorable.

But fate was against them. They had only gone

a few miles when Jens declared that he saw water ahead. Pavy at first did not believe him, but an inspection of the ice from the top of a lofty floeberg proved the correctness of the statement. Doubtless there was open water ahead, probably a good deal of it, as the opening out of new points of land revealed to the travellers that their floe was moving rather rapidly northward. Jens believed that the water extended for a considerable distance both eastward and westward; and though Pavy thought that the pack still touched Cape Joseph Henry, he dared not run counter to the greater experience of the Eskimo. Moreover, his orders were that in the event of the ice showing signs of breaking up, he was at once to make the best of his way back; so, unwillingly enough, the party faced round with the view of returning to Cape Joseph Henry. But though they travelled quickly, the water was in advance of them, and near the cape a broad lane of open sea cut them off from land, and even Pavy, unwilling as he was to return, had to admit that it was becoming desirable to do so with all convenient speed.

But how was this to be accomplished? Fortunately the ice itself solved the puzzle by closing in against Cape Joseph Henry and allowing men and dogs to scramble with the loaded sledge over the broken, hummocky floes to the ice-foot. Once on this they were safe, and fearing that the disruption of the ice might extend to Robeson Channel, they made the best of their way southward. Their fears were not groundless: at the mouth of the channel all the floes were in motion, and separated by wide lanes of open water; but further in the ice was still solid, and the journey to Fort Conger was accomplished without any difficulties greater than those which appeared to be incidental to the passage of Robeson Channel.

CHAPTER XI.

BREAKING THE ENGLISH RECORD.

DURING the absence of Pavy on his trip to Cape Joseph Henry, Lieutenant Lockwood, with a dog-sledge and four auxiliary sledges, set out for North Greenland, hoping to push his explorations beyond the furthest point reached by Lieutenant Beaumont. The plan of campaign was simple: the supporting sledges were to accompany the dog-sledge as far as Lockwood thought desirable, and from that point he, with the Eskimo Christiansen and Sergeant Brainard, would push on as far to the northward as circumstances would allow.

Greely thought that if, instead of starting with a full load, the men were, so to speak, gradually broken in to their work, more satisfactory results might be obtained. Accordingly Lockwood arranged to take up his main supply of provisions at the depôts already established, and on starting from Conger the sledges were lightly loaded with a few days' rations, the tents, cooking apparatus, and sundry other necessary articles, including a very limited supply of spare clothing. The men were all well clad in double suits of woollen underclothing, with outer garments of fur or heavy cloth, as individual taste prescribed.

On the third of April, Brainard, with the auxiliary sledges and nine men, set out from Conger in advance of Lockwood, who remained to complete his arrangements. His team consisted of eight fine dogs, and travelling quickly with a light load, he, with Christiansen and Sergeant Jewell, in a few hours reached Cape Beechy, where the advance-guard patiently awaited their arrival.

Having replenished their sledges, the explorers went on their way; but in a few hours Private Whisler complained of feeling ill, and the travellers halted for the night. But hard-frozen sleeping-bags did little to mend matters, and before morning Private Connell's foot had become frost-bitten, and Private Henry had contracted a sharp attack of rheumatism.

This was a bad beginning to the trip, and Henry was sent home. Connell did not wish to go back, and declared his ability to proceed; but in a short time he was quite knocked up, and being obviously unable to advance, was forced to submit to the inevitable, and Lockwood took charge of him to Cape Beechy, from which point he was able to go on alone.

These preliminary difficulties having been adjusted, the travellers attempted to cross Robeson Channel; but a heavy gale soon forced them to encamp, and for about five-and-forty hours kept them unwilling prisoners in their sleeping-bags. To add to their discomfort, the drifting snow made cooking impossible; and cramped, cold, and hungry, the poor fellows waited, with what patience they could summon, for the storm to cease. Windy weather, however, was just then in full swing, and at the Polaris Boat Camp the tent, being without shelter, was blown down, the men were carried off their feet, and the dog-sledge with a 200-pound load was whirled up into the air, much to the detriment of Sergeant Ralston, whom it struck on the forehead, and sent flying for a distance of several yards.

For some days violent storms prevailed, and as the tents declined to maintain a perpendicular position, the men were reduced to the necessity of ensconcing themselves in burrows in the snow. Again they were unable to cook, and privation, together with the foul air resulting from the lack of ventilation in those undesirable shelters, made several of the party ill. Two of them, Privates Whisler and Bierderbick, were so seriously affected that Lockwood dared not take them further. But ill as they were, they would not hear of any one going back with them, and helping each other as best they could, they made their way safely to Conger, where Henry and Connell had already arrived separately. Henry on his way back had fallen in with a wolf who had taken up his abode in one of the snow-houses; but he was a peaceable animal, and at once vacated his quarters in favour of the new-comer, over whose back he leaped as Henry entered the tunnel which formed the approach to the house.

While at Boat Camp the conduct of the dogs was very far from blameless: they seemed to be entirely unable to distinguish between their own and other people's property, and at one time and another purloined about forty pounds of beef and bacon; but as the depôt was well supplied, the loss was not serious. They were accomplished thieves, and on a previous occasion had made off with the meat put ready for the men's breakfast, obliging the rightful owners to content themselves with a meagre repast of biscuit.

On examining the sledges, Lockwood found that two of them were too much knocked about to be of further service. This was unlucky; but from the material a pair of spare runners and a new sledge were constructed, and the party once more went on their way, travelling by night, in order, as far as possible, to save their eyes from the perpetual glare of light.

The road certainly might have been better. In places the travelling was quite good, but here and there soft, deep snow sadly hindered the explorers, and forced them to follow the example of their predecessors on the road, and advance by means of standing pulls. The same thing happened when, as was occasionally the case, a piece of snowless ground had to be crossed; and thus, from one cause or another, it was often necessary to double-man the sledges, and traverse the same bit of road from three to five times. Another unpleasant item was the extreme cold, which kept many of the men awake for hours after they got into the sleeping-bags—a difficult and disagreeable operation in itself, when, as sometimes happened, the skins had frozen into a solid mass equally difficult to unroll and to enter.

A few days after the party left Boat Camp, another storm compelled them to halt in the shelter of some monster floebergs. The wind was blowing at the rate of nearly forty miles an hour, and the clouds of snow which drifted before it speedily buried the sledges and their loads under four feet or so of snow; but, to add to the woes of the cook, "some one had blundered," and left the alcohol for the cooker outside the tent.

Nobody was disposed to go supperless to bed, and dry biscuit without anything to drink was not an alluring prospect. The unlucky cook therefore had to turn out, and as the shovels were buried along with the alcohol, he began to burrow into the snow with his hands. It was cold work, and while thus employed he was heard to comment on Arctic expeditions in general, and on that to which he belonged in particular, in very uncomplimentary terms. But he persevered, and having at last obtained his alcohol, turned out a repast which, considering the circumstances, was voted first-rate.

In spite of difficulties and delays the explorers made good progress, and on the twenty-seventh of

April they reached Cape Bryant, where they halted for repairs. The sledges by this time were in a very dilapidated condition; two of them were unfit for further use, and Lockwood decided that the supporting party should return from this point. Necessary repairs kept the explorers in camp for a day, but on the twenty-ninth of April the sledges were again loaded; and while the homeward-bound party retraced their steps, Lockwood, Brainard, and Frederick pursued their way northward with the dog-sledge. They took with them twenty-five days' rations, including, besides the usual pemmican, musk-meat, sausage, English beef, beans, evaporated potatoes, cranberry sauce, biscuits, tea, frozen lime-juice, milk, chocolate, and sugar. These, with the tent, the cooker, a few tools and other necessary articles, and three sacks of dog-food, made up the total weight of the sledge to about 783 pounds—an average of about 98 pounds to be hauled by each dog at starting.

At first all went well, and the level floes made travelling easy and pleasant. After a few miles, however, the snow-crust softened, and the sledge occasionally broke through it, greatly to the bewilderment of the dogs. Such conduct on the part of their load was altogether outside their experience, and whenever the sledge stuck they sat down and waited calmly until their masters hauled it out for them. In some places this happened so often that the load had to be divided; but a double journey was better

BREAKING THE ENGLISH RECORD. 103

than so many stops and standing pulls, and after a time the road improved.

On one occasion a large crack in the ice was seen, and this at once suggested the idea of taking soundings. The lead-line ran out to its full length, but it was not long enough to reach the bottom. It was then supplemented by four coils of sealskin, a rope, and the dog-whip. Still the same result—no bottom—and the composite line was hauled in; but the rope broke in the operation, and the lead, the line proper to it, and the sealskin thongs were lost, thus effectually putting a stop to further investigations of this description.

On the fourth of May the travellers reached Cape Britannia, where they camped for a time to survey the locality, which, as they had now passed Beaumont's farthest point, was entirely unexplored. As far as could be seen from the summit, the cape was the south point of a fair-sized island; and to the north-east a long line of coast, broken by numerous fiords and inlets, stretched as far as the eye could reach. To the northward, however, no land appeared, and the ice held all-prevailing sway.

Having built a cairn on the top of the cape, the travellers descended, and on the following day rounded the northern point of the island. They travelled generally on the sea-ice, which was fairly level, and seemed to be of a totally different character from the heavy palæocrystic floes off Grinnell Land. In one place a pool of open water was seen, and Lockwood believed that it had for some reason remained unfrozen throughout the winter.

Progress now was fairly rapid. The dogs worked well, and the worst fault to be laid to their charge was their incurable propensity for stealing. Ritenbenk, the king-dog, was one of the worst offenders in this respect. But there was some excuse, after all, for the depredations; for the dogs were working hard on short allowance, and were, doubtless, very hungry. The fact that when Ritenbenk had successfully purloined something not a dog dared interfere with him as he devoured the coveted morsel, spoke volumes for his control over his canine subjects. Not that the dogs fared much worse than the men; for, with the view of economizing the provisions in order to extend the journey as far as possible, fifteen or more hours was now the established interval between meals. A musk-ox would have been a most pleasing addition to the stores, but though at some points numerous traces of their presence were visible, the animals themselves were conspicuously absent.

In spite of economy the provisions decreased far too rapidly to please the eager explorers, and by the thirteenth of May the state of the commissariat was such that it was decided that that day's march must be the last. Everybody wished to go as far as possible, but on this day circumstances were not propitious. First of all, a lane of open water had to be crossed; and when at some risk this had been accomplished, the explorers found themselves floundering in deep snow through which it was difficult to advance the sledge. Ten hours' labour fairly exhausted both men and dogs, and the tent was pitched on the northern point of the island. This camp was to be the limit of the outward journey; and having scrambled to the highest point attainable, and discovered their position to be 83° 24′ N., the travellers joyfully hoisted the Stars and Stripes four miles nearer to the Pole than the spot where Markham had unfurled the Union Jack six years before. England had held the palm for three hundred years, but now the United States had wrested it from her grasp, and the credit of having broken all previous records was transferred to Lockwood and Brainard.

From the foot of the flagstaff a glorious view opened out to the successful travellers. Northward the same unvarying waste of ice and snow stretched away indefinitely, unbroken by any vestige of land; but to the north-east rocky headlands and deep fiords alternated with one another for miles. To the most northern promontory visible the explorers gave the name of Cape Washington, and in another less distant headland they commemorated the gallant Kane, modestly contenting themselves with bestowing their own names respectively on the island on which they stood and on another smaller one adjacent to it. On the land side mountain ranges extended one behind the other, until the wide expanse of snow-covered inland ice blended them all together in a sheet of dazzling whiteness.

There was no object in making a long stay on Lockwood Island, even supposing that the commissariat would have admitted of such a course, and on the evening of the sixteenth of May the explorers turned their faces homewards. The journey was, on the whole, uneventful, and the principal excitement was due to the dogs, who, being on very short commons, endeavoured to supply deficiencies by unauthorized attacks on anything that could be gnawed. Once, having pulled the ammunition-bag to pieces, they endeavoured to make a meal of its contents; and though the cartridges were beyond the powers of even an Eskimo dog, about a dozen were chawed up and rendered unfit for their legitimate use.

Though a couple of pairs of snow-shoes had been brought from Fort Conger, on the outward journey they had not been used, having been cached with other spare articles at Cape Britannia. On the return of the party they were unearthed, and Lockwood and Brainard having taken them into use, thenceforth skimmed easily over snow into which Christiansen, who was minus these aids to locomotion, frequently sank to his hips.

So rapidly did the party advance, that at Cape Bryant Lockwood was able to make a small depôt of provisions for the use of future parties. Then

RETURN OF LOCKWOOD TO FORT CONGER.   Page 107.

pursuing their way to Repulse Harbour, they opened Beaumont's cairn, and found the record of his terrible journey over the same ground so prosperously traversed by themselves. It was a mournful story of suffering bravely borne, and ended with the pathetic words: "We cannot hope to reach Polaris Bay without assistance—two men cannot do it; so we will go as far as we can, and live as long as we can. God help us!"

But no such hardships fell to the lot of the Americans, and in a few hours they safely reached Boat Camp, where they found Sergeants Lynn, Ralston, and Elison awaiting them. All spare provisions were cached, and then the whole party set out, and crossed Robeson Channel in fourteen hours. The day happened to be a dull one, so the goggles were discarded—an indiscretion which led to unpleasant results, for several of the travellers were struck with snow-blindness. Two of them became totally unable to see, and had to be ignominiously conducted home by their comrades.

This was the only drawback to a most successful trip. Sixty days of hard work and privation seemed to have had no ill effects whatever, and on the first of June, when the explorers reached Conger, with the exception of this temporary injury to their eyes, they were all sound in wind and limb.

CHAPTER XII.

GRINNELL LAND LAKES.

TOWARDS the end of April Lieutenant Greely, with Privates Bender, Connell, and Whisler, started on an excursion into the interior of Grinnell Land. The first part of the route lay along the shore, and three or four marches brought them to a point which, until they reached it, appeared to be the end of Conybeare Inlet; but they soon saw that it was nothing of the kind, and that beyond it a long, narrow fiord, bordered by inaccessible cliffs, ran inland for several miles. Further on this fiord branched, and one arm which ran north-west looked so tempting that Greely decided to explore it; but before striking off from the main fiord, he wished to find out how much further it extended. It was needless for all to go on this errand, so he left the men to prepare lunch, and went on alone.

An hour's rapid walking brought him to a landlocked and almost circular bay, bounded on the south and west by gently-sloping shores, which presented a marked contrast to the lofty rocky cliffs which had hitherto prevailed. Travelling over the low-lying ground promised to be easy enough, but Greely reserved the investigation of this locality for a future occasion, and turning his back on Ida Bay, as he named his new discovery, he rejoined his companions, and after lunch the journey up the northern branch of the fiord began.

Before long the colour of the ice changed from opaque white to a delicate blue, which indicated that salt water had given place to fresh. This fresh-water ice rested on a substratum of sea-ice, and a little further on the explorers came to a frozen dam, fifteen feet or so in height, which had formed at the point where a river which here debouched into the fiord met the tidal water. Over this dam streams trickled from the pent-in river behind, and these, freezing as they ran, gradually raised the ice-barrier and produced the curious combination of ice below.

Beyond the dam the river-ice was smooth for some miles, but higher up the water was unfrozen, and ran merrily down between high walls of clear ice. Advancing further, the explorers found that the river issued from a frozen lake, whose snowy surface, stretching away for miles on either side of the stream, flashed back the sunshine glorified into gem-like flashes of many-coloured light. Beyond the glittering lake ranges of low hills, for the most part clear of snow, made a foreground to the loftier snow-clad peaks, which stretched away into the dim distance till the eye could no longer follow them. Fairyland itself could not have been more beautiful.

Around the lake, wherever the ground was clear of snow, dwarf willows, grass, and flowers abounded, and a good many musk-oxen and hares were seen. Beasts and birds were quite fearless; several ptarmigan came fearlessly to inspect the visitors, and to decide what manner of beings they were, and one even perched on the tent-pole close to Connell's head.

Crossing the lake, to which Greely gave the name of Lake Hazen, the travellers found themselves confronted by a magnificent glacier. This, in honour of Mrs. Greely, was dubbed Henrietta Nesmith Glacier, and Greely spent several hours in examining it. The next morning Bender made an attempt to scale one of the neighbouring peaks; but at every step the soft sands which covered it caused him to slip back, and he had to give up the attempt.

Time would not allow of a long stay, for should a thaw begin the difficulties of the return journey would be greatly increased, so after this very cursory investigation the camp was broken up. A single march took the party to Ruggles River, as they had named the stream, and the next day they proceeded homewards—none too soon, as Bender, who was sent back to fetch some forgotten articles, reported that the ice had begun to break up. Haste was evidently desirable, but the rapid rate at which they travelled reduced some of the party to a rather dilapidated condition, and finally Connell was seized with such severe cramp that it was all he could do to hobble along. He refused to get on to the sledge; but about half a mile from home, Greely met Dr. Pavy and Jens with the dog-sledge, and promptly despatched them to fetch in the invalid, who was painfully toiling along in the rear.

Later in the summer, Greely, accompanied by Lynn, Salor, Bierderbick, and Whisler, again visited Lake Hazen. This time instead of sledges they used a small wheeled vehicle, and varied their route by travelling *viâ* Black Rock Vale, a long gorge which opened on Discovery Bay. A single march brought them to Lake Heintzelmann, whose ice-bound waters extended from side to side of the narrow valley, and near to which a couple of trees were found embedded in the earth. As nothing of the kind or size grew in the neighbourhood, it was evident they had been carried by water to the position they now occupied, and on these premises Greely concluded that at no distant period the sea had extended far up the valley; in which opinion he was confirmed by the discovery of numerous marine shells around the lake. Almost all signs of winter had disappeared, and grass, willows, saxifrage, and other plants grew in profusion, affording abundant fuel for cooking purposes. Life of all kinds seemed abundant; both fur and feather were represented. Butterflies darted hither and thither, and lazy-looking bumble-bees hummed leisurely from plant to plant. Flies, too, abounded, and were unremitting in their attentions to the new-comers, whom they pestered unmercifully.

The road was very bad; but as some of the stores were bestowed in knapsacks, by changing the work as the haulers and knapsack-carriers respectively became tired fair progress was made, and in due time the travellers crossed the watershed, and after passing several smaller sheets of water, reached Lake Hazen, where everything had put on its summer dress. The ground seemed to be comparatively fertile, but no sign of the presence of human beings was to be seen, though it was evident that Eskimos had inhabited the locality, for several ruined huts were discovered. Some of these which seemed to have been permanent residences were carefully examined, and a number of articles—combs, fish-hooks, domestic utensils, etc.—were discovered and annexed.

Every day the sun gained power, and by the time Ruggles River was reached the thermometer stood at 73°. This was too warm to be pleasant for men clad in garments suited for a much lower temperature, and the heat added not a little to the labour of hauling the wagon, which by this time was in a very shaky condition. Frequent repairs were necessary, and as these caused a good deal of delay, Greely, who had already sent back Salor and Whisler, declined to have anything more to do with the defective vehicle. Each man, therefore, took as much as he could conveniently carry, and leaving the wagon where it could easily be seen, the explorers trudged along the shore of the lake, though the snow on the surrounding hills, melted by the heat of the sun, had formed numerous ice-cold streams only to be crossed at the expense of soaked clothing, which there was no means of changing. Between cold and overwork Bierderbick became quite knocked up, and shortly after reaching the end of the lake he was obliged to relinquish the idea of going further. He declared, however, that he could make his way back to Conger alone; and having seen him off, Greely and Lynn pushed on up a river which debouched into the end of Lake Hazen, and to which Greely gave the name of Very. In some places the travelling was exceedingly bad, and it was not improved by heavy rains, which several times forced the two explorers to take refuge in their wet sleeping-bags, and in damp wretchedness await finer weather.

On the fourth of July they reached the foot of a lofty peak, to which they gave the name of Mount Arthur. The temptation to climb it was too strong to be resisted; but after floundering for some time through deep, half-melted snow, Lynn was forced to return. Greely would not give in, and sending Lynn back he struggled on alone to the summit, though before he reached it he was obliged to stop to gain breath after every few steps; and for all that he could feel of his nearly-frozen feet, they might as well have been blocks of wood.

The peak was one of the loftiest in the country, and a glorious view rewarded his exertions. Mountain chains stretched away in all directions—the low hills bare of snow, while the higher ranges were clad in the white mantle which in all probability shrouded them perpetually. It was evident that it would be impossible to go far enough to learn more than he could see from his present vantage-ground, and having assured himself of this, Greely returned to Lynn, and the two retraced their steps to their last camping-place, and thence began the homeward journey. Reduced loads allowed them to travel rapidly, and they soon reached Ruggles River. But here their troubles began. Since they last crossed it the stream had risen, and now ran so swiftly that they had difficulty in fording it; and a heavy downpour of rain, which began soon after they crossed the stream, continued almost without intermission for eight days. To make matters worse, the ground over which they were travelling was rough and stony, and as hard wear and perpetual soaking had by this time reduced the travellers' shoes to a worse than useless condition, every step was a penance. But they plodded doggedly on, and though in crossing the deep stream which drained Lake Heintzelmann they were almost swept away by the current, the journey was safely accomplished, albeit by the time they reached Conger both men were almost worn out.

CHAPTER XIII.

GLACIERS AND ICE-FIELDS.

DURING the absence of the sledge-parties life went on very quietly at Conger. The observers were pretty fully occupied with scientific matters, and the rest of the party employed themselves with hunting and short sledging trips. Gardening was another source of interest; but Long, who acted as head-gardener, was not particularly successful, as even lettuces and radishes declined to grow. He obtained better results as a cattle-rearer; for four musk-calves having been brought in by the hunters who had shot the rest of the herd, Long took them in hand, and the little fellows soon became quite tame. The puppies, too, had grown and prospered. They were now big enough to take a share in the work, and Schneider, who had the care of them, was very proud of his five-month-old charges when they successfully accomplished a trip of fifty miles in twenty hours.

Greely had hoped to be visited by a relief-ship during the summer, and one or two trips were made by Pavy and others to the mouth of Lady Franklin Sound, and even as far as Carl Ritter Bay, in the hope of meeting with the much-desired vessel. But no signs of her were to be seen, and as it became clear that for that season all hope of her arrival must be abandoned, the party resigned themselves as best they could to another year without news of the great world outside Discovery Harbour.

The absence of news and of letters from home was, however, only a part of the inconvenience arising from the non-arrival of the relief-ship. Counting on its making its appearance with fresh supplies, Greely had hitherto in no way stinted the use of any of the stores, and, in consequence, of such articles as vegetables and flour only the bare regulation allowance remained. This necessitated some care in the use of the said edibles; but that this necessary economy might give as little annoyance as possible, special pains were taken to vary the cooking. As autumn approached the house was overhauled; defects noted during the last winter were remedied, and all means were employed to make the second winter at Conger pass even more comfortably than its predecessor had done.

The chief sufferers from the approach of winter were the musk-calves. As the light decreased their strength diminished, and by the end of the first week in October all four had come to an untimely end. About the same time the only bear which visited Conger made his appearance. The sportsmen, of course, turned out to meet him, but they were unable to get to close quarters; and after roaming around for a day or two he came to the conclusion that the locality was not healthy for him, and made tracks for a neighbourhood where his tenure of life might be less insecure. Other hunting operations were more successful. A good deal of game of one kind and another was secured, and Jens caught two foxes alive. One of these continued so vicious that his execution was ordered; but the other, named Reuben, grew quite tame, though he never became altogether friendly with the dogs. He remained for some time a member of the party, but eventually the restraints of civilized society began to pall, and he made himself a burrow in the snow.

The winter passed uneventfully, and as in the preceding year, the return of daylight ushered in the greatest cold of the season: it was curious that in both years the lowest temperature was registered on the fourth of February. A few days later one of the puppies was brought in gasping for breath, and with his tail frozen stiff—he seemed to be altogether in a bad way; but the frozen tail was judiciously thawed in cold water, and in time he recovered his wonted health and vivacity. Otherwise all went well, and with the exception of Bierderbick, who for a time suffered somewhat from rheumatism, nobody seemed much the worse for the cold and darkness.

Lockwood was the first to take the field, and on

the tenth of March, with Brainard and four others, he set out for Cape Sumner, where he cached a stack of provisions for use on his next trip, which would, he hoped, carry him far beyond his record point. This hope was, however, destined to disappointment, for when he reached Black Horn Cliffs he found further progress barred: a belt of open water cut off the sea-ice from the shore, and though Lockwood managed to scale a glacier which presented the least impracticable route to the summit of the cliffs, it was utterly impossible to haul up the sledges. After waiting for a few days, the explorers were rewarded by seeing ice form over the water, and as soon as there was a chance of its bearing they essayed to reach the pack beyond. But they had not gone far when the ice broke up and began to drift off-shore. One or two of the dogs fell into the water, and seeing the danger Lockwood shouted to Christiansen to go back to land with the sledges while he ran after Brainard, who was some distance ahead selecting the road. The Eskimo, however, was not to be outdone in generosity, and whipping up his dogs he dashed past Lockwood, overtook Brainard, and the whole party reached land in safety. It was a close shave: so fast did the ice move that by the time Brainard had been overtaken a water-lane several yards in width had opened along the shore, and dogs and men scrambled to land as best they could over a block of ice which had drifted against a grounded floeberg.

GLACIERS AND ICE-FIELDS. 119

On his return from this trip Lockwood found at Repulse Harbour a Union Jack which Beaumont had been compelled to abandon. He brought it back to Conger, and through all the vicissitudes which afterwards befell the expedition it was carefully cherished, and finally was transmitted to its own country, where it found a resting-place among other national relics in the Naval Museum at Greenwich.

Lockwood would gladly have tried his luck again in Greenland, but Greely considered that his energies would be better employed in further exploring Grinnell Land. Accordingly, on the twenty-fifth of April, he set out with Brainard, Christiansen, and the best dog-team, taking a small extra sledge and a couple of knapsacks in addition to the usual equipment. Four marches took the explorers to the head of Ella Bay, the southern of the two branches into which Archer Fiord divides. This point was about sixty-seven miles from Conger, and here Lockwood camped while he examined the locality. But a short investigation manifested the impossibility of a further advance by this route; for the valley was completely filled by a glacier, hemmed in on either side by magnificent cliffs. Nor was the surrounding country more promising: when Lockwood and Brainard viewed it from the summit of a cliff more than 4,400 feet in height, nothing was to be seen but snow-shrouded mountains and valleys, interspersed here and there with glaciers; so they wisely concluded to transfer their base of operations to Beatrix Bay, the northern branch of the fiord.

This promised well, but the travelling soon became so bad that the large sledge was discarded in favour of the small one, which the dogs could draw even over mountainous country. This was loaded with eleven days' rations and a few other indispensable articles; and having left all the heavy articles in a cache, the travellers started to make their way through a cañon so rough and rugged that the sledge speedily collapsed, but the expenditure of a little time and ingenuity restored it to working order. In deference to its incapacity, some of the provisions and a few other things were cached to be picked up on the return journey, and another march carried the explorers to the top of what Lockwood thought was undoubtedly the water-divide of Grinnell Land. The camp was pitched 1,200 feet above sea-level, but at the distance of a mile or two the land attained more than double that elevation.

A wonderful view now unfolded itself. Southward of the camp the land was covered with an ice-cap which faced the explorers in the guise of a solid wall of ice. It followed the configuration of the country in a manner which so forcibly reminded Lockwood of the Great Wall of China that he named the ice-field the Chinese Wall Glacier—a title which was afterwards discarded in favour of the more ambitious name of " Mer de Glace Agassiz." The ice seemed to cover the ground to an enormous depth, and apparently extended across Grinnell Land from sea to sea, being evidently connected with the glacier above Archer Fiord. Northward of the ice-wall the country was diversified by lakes and mountain peaks, while the ground in front of the glacier had a general northward slope.

Two marches down a steep narrow valley brought the travellers to the head of an arm of the sea which received the name of Greely Fiord, and into which more than one glacier discharged itself. Provisions by this time were getting scarce, but by putting an interval of nineteen hours between meals, the travellers contrived to find time to explore about twenty-six miles of the newly-discovered fiord, the total length of which seemed to be more than sixty miles. From a high cliff near the furthest camp a view of the mouth was obtained, and the capes on the north and south were named respectively, after their discoverers, Brainard and Lockwood. Two or three days were spent in exploring the neighbourhood of the camp, collecting fossils, and making various observations; but the state of the commissariat forbade a longer stay, and the homeward journey began. The sledge-load was now greatly reduced; but light as it was, the half-famished dogs could hardly scale the defile and the final snow-ridge, beyond which the large sledge and the stores had been left. Yard after yard they made their way upward—panting, struggling, almost exhausted; for they, as well as the men, had been on short commons for some time, and now the last scrap of their provisions had been eaten. But they reached the camping-place somehow, and there, in the absence of other food, Lockwood was obliged to kill one of the weakest dogs. The meal thus provided enabled the others to go on, and in three marches the explorers reached the head of Beatrix Bay, where they had cached some provisions for the homeward journey. But in their ravenous condition the supply was quite insufficient, more especially as on arriving at Simmons Bay Lockwood made a side trip up an adjacent valley, where he discovered a lake of considerable size.

After making this discovery the travellers pushed on along the fiord in the direction of home, which was still too far off for their comfort. The dogs were growing weaker and weaker, and though Christiansen one day killed a seal, the meat did not go very far towards supplying human and canine needs; and when within sight of Conger, one of the dogs became so exhausted that he could go no further. He was at once unharnessed; but it was too late to save him, and in a few minutes he died, having, like the immortal Jim Bludso, "done his level best."

CHAPTER XIV.

RETREATING.

THE non-arrival of the ship in 1882 caused Greely some anxiety, for he could not hide from himself the possibility that some unforeseen cause might again prevent the vessel from reaching Conger. In view of such a contingency, his instructions provided that the situation should be abandoned not later than September 1, 1883, and that the retreating party should proceed southward by boat, until they either fell in with a ship or reached Littleton Island, where a large depôt had been established. With the view of saving time and trouble should a retreat become necessary, as soon as the light permitted the men set to work to convey stores to Cape Baird, at the mouth of Lady Franklin Sound, and an ice-boat which Beaumont had abandoned at Polaris Bay was fetched by Rice and laid up near the depôt. Having finished this work, the men occupied themselves in collecting natural history and botanical specimens, and Brainard and Gardiner gathered together a large assortment of fossils. All these collections were duly classified and arranged, and Greely, with an assistant, spent a great deal of time in putting in order the records of the many scientific observations taken during the year.

Still no vessel appeared, and on the ninth of August the long-contemplated retreat began. It was impossible to take the dogs, and as every one was unwilling to kill them, several barrels of blubber, pork, beef, and bread were opened for their benefit. A quantity of coal, the natural history collections, and sundry stores were also left, and the men, taking with them the few personal belongings that could be allowed, embarked in the steam-launch and the boats to begin their battle with the ice. After twenty-four hours' hard work they reached Cape Baird, but only to find that a heavy gale was blowing, and that they must resign themselves to further delay. There was, however, plenty to do in transferring the stores from the depôt to the boats; and soon after this was accomplished the wind dropped, and the launch steamed off, towing behind her three large boats and one small one, all of them heavily laden.

Having rounded the point, the launch was in open water, and for a while all looked promising; but the ice, uncertain as usual, soon blocked the way, and the men camped for the night on the ice-foot. By the morning the wind had changed, and the ice, in consequence, so far opened that it was possible to go on. This kind of navigation continued for several days, and to make things more disagreeable, the weather was seldom fine: fogs and snow-storms took it by turns to chill the explorers, until their damp clothes and cramped limbs converted the boats into veritable places of torment.

On the thirteenth of August a heavy pack was encountered, and after awaiting developments for an hour or two, Sergeant Brainard took the small boat and went to examine a monster floeberg which had grounded some distance from the shore. At first sight it seemed to block the way entirely, but a closer inspection revealed a narrow chasm extending right through the monster berg. It was just wide enough to admit the launch; and having passed through these iron gates, the boats were in open water. But they had not gone far when the ice again stopped them, and held them prisoners for nearly a week. The time, however, was not wasted. Lieutenant Kislingbury, who was a most enthusiastic hunter, went ashore with Christiansen, and travelling up a narrow valley which ran at right angles to the coast, he discovered several lakes, to which he gave his name.

By the eighteenth of August everybody was heartily tired of waiting, and as the ice would not open voluntarily, Greely determined to force a way through it. Four hours' hard work opened a passage, and after one or two more delays the boats safely reached Cape Joseph Good. Kennedy Channel was now well astern, but at the next point the ice closed in, and the men barely managed to drag the launch into a position where a slight break in the ice-foot protected her from the heaviest pressure of the pack. One of the smaller boats was hauled on to a floe, and the other two found a refuge in slight indentations of the ice-foot until such time as, under the united influences of wind and tide, the ice saw fit to release its prisoners and allow them to advance to Cape Collinson. Here Nares had established a depôt, and Greely desired Lockwood to annex the stores, consisting of meat, bread, salt, pepper, onion-powder, and fuel.

Cold weather unfortunately set in early. Already new ice formed every night, and the probability of finding a ship, or even of reaching Littleton Island, became daily more remote, for after many minor hindrances the pack closed in around the boats; but the men still hoped against hope, and for several days they waited patiently. Occasionally a seal was shot, and though a short time before seal-meat had not been by any means a popular edible, everybody was now glad enough to eat it, and even to drink the blood.

On the eighth of September the mercury sank below zero, thus giving a final blow to all hopes of the ice breaking up; and the next day Greely decided to abandon the boats and travel over the ice with sledges, one or two of which had been recently made. All hands now busied themselves in making preparations for a start: the launch and a couple of boats were secured on the ice; the other two boats with the stores were loaded up on the sledges, and on the tenth of September the march began. Excluding the sledges, the weight to be drawn amounted to about 7,000 pounds — a heavy load for twenty-five men even had the travelling been good, and with deep snow and rough ice it was necessary to go many times over the same ground. The selection of the route was committed to Brainard; but even the most carefully-chosen path presented so many difficulties that, after a couple of days' experience of hauling two boats, it was unanimously agreed that one of them should be left behind. Even then progress was slow and hardships were many; the men were sometimes almost too tired to move; and one night when, after an extra hard day's work, they camped on a big floe, everybody was too tired to take the trouble even to pitch the tent.

In the morning the wind was so violent that travelling was out of the question, and cooking presented insuperable difficulties. Pemmican and cold water were not attractive fare, nor were wet, snowy sleeping-bags comfortable resting-places; but circumstances would allow of nothing better during the two or three days that the gale continued. The only consoling circumstance was the steady southward drift of the ice, which by the twenty-fifth of September had carried the party near to Brevoort Island. Dr. Pavy thought it might be possible to reach land, but in this view nobody coincided; and that evening another gale drove the pack down upon the explorers' floe with such force that, despite its fifty feet of thickness, it split in several directions. One of the cracks thus opened swallowed up part of an ice-house, and another opened almost under the feet of the men who were rolling up the tent. About fifty feet distant was another large floe, with which some closely-packed rubble-ice formed a rather unstable connection; but for the time being it was crossable, and with wonderful dispatch the men scrambled over the perilous bridge, dragging with them their possessions of every description, and reaching the solid ice just as the floes began to separate.

Two more days of cold, hunger, and wretchedness had to be endured before the weather moderated sufficiently to allow the retreating explorers to go on to Cape Hawks, where they hoped that a ship might be awaiting them. But again disappointment was their lot: no sign of human life broke the Arctic stillness, and when Rice examined the cairn on Washington Irving Island, he found that it had not been visited since the *Proteus* had called there in 1881. There was little chance that so late in the season any relief-ship would go so far north, and it only remained for the retreating explorers to push on, if possible, to Littleton Island. Before leaving Cape Hawks, however, a depôt which Nares had established there was

BREAKING UP OF THE ICE. *Page 128.*

inspected; but it did not contain much, and what there was, was in bad condition and almost uneatable.

A few miles to the south of Cape Hawks another deadlock occurred; but the ice continued to drift slowly southward, and in time it brought the floe on which the explorers were encamped into Baird Inlet. Land was now not far distant, and on the following day they effected a landing on a rocky coast free from any ice-foot. The next business was to find a place suitable for winter quarters; and then, as no depôt was discovered in the neighbourhood, on the first of October Rice and Jens set out for Cape Sabine, where supplies were known to have been cached.

Meanwhile the rest of the party occupied themselves in house-building. Sergeant Gardiner had severely injured his finger during the retreat, and this unfitted him for heavy work; but every one else was busily employed, and in spite of the difficulties, which were greatly increased by the absence of building tools, the work went on so prosperously that on the night of the sixth of October the worn-out men slept under cover, with moss for their bed. This was, at any rate, an improvement on lying out on the floe; and when sufficient moss had been collected to stop up crevices in the walls and roof, the hut really was, by comparison, comfortable. Food, however, was terribly scarce, and in order to make the supplies hold out, it was necessary to reduce the daily rations to six ounces of bread, twelve ounces of meat, two and a half ounces of potatoes, with one ounce of extract of beef, while the tea suffered such reduction that on one occasion when the cook omitted to put any tea into the pot, the omission was not discovered until some time afterwards. The best hope of getting through the winter lay in obtaining a supply of meat, and Kislingbury, Long, Jens, and Christiansen, the most experienced hunters of the party, spent the greater part of their time in scouring the neighbourhood in search of game. A couple of walruses, could they have been procured, would have practically removed all anxieties connected with the commissariat; but though plenty were seen, they carefully kept to the open water, far out of reach of the hunters.

On the ninth of October, Rice and Jens returned from Cape Sabine. They had discovered three depôts, containing in all from 10,000 to 12,000 pounds of stores; and they had also found a record left a few weeks before by the *Proteus*, containing the welcome intelligence: "Your friends are all well." So far the news brought by the two scouts was good; but another letter, from Lieutenant Garlington, the officer in charge of the relief expedition, gave tidings of a disaster. The *Proteus* had been crushed by the ice on the twenty-fourth of July, and had gone down so suddenly that there had been little time to land stores, and much of her cargo was in consequence lost. Her crew, however, were all safe, and had gone south, hoping to meet with a vessel, as one or two steamers were known to be on their way northward at the time. The letter gave a great deal of information of various depôts which were said to have been established at Cape Sabine and Littleton Island, and concluded with the reassuring words: "Everything within the power of man will be done to rescue the brave men at Fort Conger from their perilous position."

CHAPTER XV.

STARVING AT SABINE.

LIEUTENANT GARLINGTON'S letter led Greely to believe that help was already on the way, but circumstances beyond the control of that officer prevented the arrival of the expected succour. If Greely had had an idea of the real state of affairs, he would at any cost have continued his southward journey; but as it was, in the daily expectation that a ship would arrive, he decided to transfer the camp to the neighbourhood of Cape Sabine. The plan was not without its drawbacks, for there was less game at Sabine than around Baird Inlet; but, on the other hand, with the available hauling power it would be simply impossible to transport the stores cached at Cape Sabine to the present camp, and on the eleventh of October the move was begun.

The position chosen for the new camp was on the shore of a small lake not far from the spot where Garlington had cached the few stores saved from the wreck. The spot was undesirable in some respects, for high hills shut out the rays of the sun several days before that luminary sank below the horizon; but it was, on the whole, the best place that could be found, and numerous scattered boulders and extensive snow-drifts offered exceptional facilities for building.

It was most desirable to get under cover quickly, so with the exception of Long and the Eskimos who were still occupied in hunting, all hands betook themselves to architectural pursuits—some cutting and hauling snow-blocks, fetching sand for the floor and stones for the walls, and others constructing the edifice. When completed, thick stone walls, well banked with snow, and three feet or so in height, supported the whale-boat, which with sundry oars and ropes, supplemented by blocks of snow, served as a roof. Fuel was terribly scarce—there would be no good fires at Camp Clay, as the new shelter was called—and for greater warmth the door was approached through a snow tunnel from which the storehouse also opened. It was a wretched den, but the travellers were hopeful and cheery as ever, and worked hard, as long as daylight lasted, in hunting and hauling stores from the depôts to the camp.

The result could hardly be considered satisfactory, in spite of the pluck shown in the work by all, and especially by Long, who, though far from being a strong man, camped out in the cold for days at a stretch in an almost futile attempt to obtain game. This failure was most serious, especially as some of the stores found in the depôts were so much damaged by wet as to be unfit for use; though when some rotten and mouldy dog-biscuit was brought up from one of the depôts, some of the men in their ravenous hunger began forthwith to devour it. Poor fellows! they might well be hungry, for on the first of November the daily ration was reduced to about six ounces of biscuit, four ounces of meat, and four ounces of vegetables. This, according to Pavy, was not enough to support life; but everybody else agreed cheerfully to the reduction, knowing that with a more generous diet it would be impossible that the provisions should hold out.

One chance of increasing the rations still remained. Nares had left a cache supposed to contain about 144 pounds of meat at Cape Isabella, forty miles to the southward. Could this be fetched up? Rice, Lynn, Frederick, and Elison volunteered to do their best, and on the second of November they started with a light sledge, a few necessaries for camping out, and a daily allowance of food, augmented for the occasion to half a pound of biscuit and the same amount of meat.

Four days' hard travelling, with ever-increasing darkness added to the difficulties of the way, brought the four men to Cape Isabella. Climbing to the summit they gazed around, and by the light of the moon saw, stretching away to the southward, a vast extent of blue water, which, could they but have reached it with their boats, would have enabled the castaways to reach a place of safety. Well, it was no use to cry over spilt milk. They could not get either boats or stores to the sea; so turning their backs on those tempting waves, the men loaded up their sledge with the meat and set out for Camp Clay.

The additional weight was too much for their strength, and they travelled so slowly that by the time they reached their last camp Elison's hands and feet were badly frozen. Very little could be done to relieve him; even the sleeping-bag was hard as iron; but when, with much difficulty, they managed to crawl into it, Elison was put in the middle, and Frederick and Rice, taking a hand apiece, tried to thaw them with the warmth of their own limbs.

In the morning the sledgers were early astir; but Elison, now most susceptible to cold, was soon as bad as ever, and as he could scarcely walk, Frederick was forced to support him behind the sledge, which the others hauled as best they could until their strength failed. Sadly against their will, they had to leave the meat behind, with a rifle stuck up in the snow beside it to mark its resting-place. Thus relieved of the heaviest part of their load they travelled on manfully, and at length reached the spot originally selected for winter quarters.

A fire was kindled, and again poor Elison, now worse frost-bitten than before, was thawed. He spent a wretched night—indeed no one had much rest; but when morning came it merely brought a renewal of labour and suffering. All the available strength was now needed at the drag-ropes, so Elison, who seemed unable to guide himself, was tied to the sledge behind which he stumbled along, often falling and being dragged for some yards before his friends discovered his plight. At length they could go no further, and regardless of a biting gale which made it impossible to light a fire, three of them crawled into their bag; while Rice, the strongest of the party, made his way to Camp Clay, fifteen miles distant, to obtain help.

Frederick and his companions meanwhile were, if possible, in worse plight than before; for after a few hours the bag froze so hard that its occupants were unable to stir. When the relief-party arrived on the scene, they had been for eighteen hours in one position, half-frozen, hungry, thirsty, and miserable; and in order to release them the bag had to be cut to pieces. Frederick and Lynn soon came round, but Elison by this time was barely alive, and though under Dr. Pavy's care he partially recovered, his feet and the greater part of his hands had to be amputated. His sufferings were terrible, but his bright, cheery spirit helped to carry him on, and after the first few days he rarely uttered a word of complaint.

After the return of Rice's party from Cape Isabella, day succeeded day in dreary wretchedness, to which scarcity of fuel added yet further misery. The coal had long been exhausted, and nothing combustible remained except a small supply of stearine and alcohol, a portion of the whale-boat, and a little birchwood. Almost all of these caused clouds of smoke, and though several tomato-tins were ingeniously converted into a chimney, so much dense smoke made its escape into the hut, that while cooking was in progress it was only at rare intervals that anybody could see the man next to him.

Time passed but slowly. In the darkness of winter little or no work was possible, and as hour after hour the men lay idle in their bags, every scrap of printed paper, items of news, statistics, army regulations—anything and everything was read and re-read; and Greely gave daily lectures on the physical geography and productions of the United States, which others supplemented by descriptions of their life and adventures under sunnier skies. Several times during the winter foxes were shot—their average weight was about four pounds; and though a fox, when spread over a week, made an almost microscopic addition to each man's daily allowance, things had reached a pitch at which even a half-ounce of food was not to be despised. A few weeks of this miserable existence completely demoralized some of the men, and one or two were unable to resist the temptation, when occasion offered, to purloin food from the general store, or from one or other of their comrades. One of the chief offenders in this respect was Private Henry, who was more than once caught in the act of stealing; but such cases were quite the exception, and by far the greater number bore their privations bravely and cheerfully. In the face of these thefts, however, it became necessary to issue stringent orders that, with the exception of Brainard, who was in charge of the supplies, nobody was to enter the storehouse.

As time went on, though Elison slowly improved, several others became ill, among them Kislingbury and Lockwood. The former had received a serious internal injury while out one day with the sledge, and the latter was suffering from the terrible cold and starvation, which, slowly but surely, were undermining his strength.

Christmas came at length. Everybody had been saving up something, in order that the occasion might be a festive one; and as a few extra supplies were issued at dinner-time, there was *nearly* enough to eat. The evening was spent in quite a jovial manner with songs and stories, while the hilarity was further increased by a bowl of mild punch.

Towards the middle of January, as Brainard reported that the supply of biscuit was greater than had been supposed, half an ounce extra was issued daily—a most popular measure, and one which was greatly needed, for by slow degrees starvation was doing its cruel work. Lockwood was becoming alarmingly weak: he could hardly sit up alone, and often wandered in his talk. He and several others had been forbidden by the doctor to smoke, and the forced abstention from his pipe was a terrible deprivation to the hapless lieutenant. Unfortunately he was not the only invalid. Cross, though still at work splitting wood for the stove, was in even worse condition, and the doctor believed that he was suffering from scurvy. He and the other sick had a most unselfish nurse in Bierderbick, who gave almost all his time and attention to them. But in spite of his care, Cross suddenly became worse. Brandy and soup were given to him; but he sank rapidly, and died on the evening of the eighteenth of January, nominally of dropsy, though probably "starvation" would have been the truer word. A shallow grave was dug on the hill above the camp, and when Greely had read the burial service in the hut the funeral procession set out. The military honour of a salute would willingly have been accorded to the dead man, but consideration for the needs of the living forbade the needless expenditure of any ammunition.

The death of Cross, occurring so unexpectedly, had naturally a depressing effect on his comrades. Lockwood practically lost hope, and one day he begged Greely to leave him behind with his share of the provisions whenever it became possible to attempt to reach Littleton Island, as he considered that in his weak condition he would not only be unable to cross Smith Sound himself, but that his presence would hinder the others. Greely, of course, refused to do anything of the kind, and a slight increase in the allowance of bread had quite an exhilarating effect upon Lockwood, though he still continued terribly weak, and his mind did not altogether recover its balance. Brainard, too, began to show signs of serious illness; but in spite of the doctor's directions to avoid cold and hard work, he quite refused to give up any of his duties.

As the light increased, preparations were made for travelling, and Greely began to feed up Rice and Jens, who were to make a preliminary trip to Littleton Island.

They set out on the second of February, leaving everybody hopeful; but after four days' absence they reappeared at the camp, having been prevented by open water from reaching their destination. Their failure was disappointing; but it was not yet too late for a good sharp frost to close the strait and render sledge-travelling possible. Hope, therefore, still flourished, though the men could not hide from themselves the fact that should the frost not come their position would be a most critical one, since, weakened as they were by long privation, it would be impossible for them to remove the long-boat from the roof and transport it to the water's edge.

CHAPTER XVI.

FAITHFUL UNTO DEATH.

THE first of March, the day on which Greely had promised himself that the party should start for Littleton Island, at length arrived; but still the strait was open, and the men, who daily lost strength, knew that they were now more unable than before to launch the boat. If only there had been ice all the way, they believed themselves strong enough to cross; but to freeze seemed to be about the last thing the strait intended to do, and so in anxious waiting the days rolled away, each one lessening the chances of escape as the supply of food diminished. By the end of the first week of March the milk, soup, blubber, vegetables, and dog-biscuit were used up; and though the hunters were constantly afoot, their best exertions produced pitifully small results.

Distant hunting trips were seldom attempted, but on the tenth of March, Long and Christiansen set out along the shore to Alexandra Harbour, which Nares and Feilden had reported to be abundantly stocked with game. Hitherto the coast in this district had not been explored, and ever mindful of the objects of the expedition, Greely directed the men to pay attention to geographical discovery as well as to hunting. " Game in any event, but new lands when possible," said the energetic lieutenant.

On reaching Alexandra Harbour, the hunters found that an ice-cap covered the greater part of the surrounding country. This was not promising for the main object of the trip, and in spite of diligent search, neither fur nor feather rewarded their exertions; and though they saw in the distance several new capes, geographical zeal did not prevent them becoming thoroughly worn out. To go further seemed useless, and the two made a futile attempt to insinuate themselves into their hard-frozen sleeping-bag. Finding it impervious to their efforts, they made some tea, and continued their march for an hour, and then, tired out, made another attempt to camp. This time they managed to get partly into the bag; but Long was shortly afterwards seized with severe cramp, and Christiansen having brought him round with a mixture of hot rum and ammonia, unselfishly gave up the whole bag to the sick man, remaining outside in the cold himself. The rest and warmth so obtained completed Long's restoration, and he was able to return to Camp Clay.

The failure to obtain game was very disappointing, as the stores were all but exhausted. But Brainard was not yet at the end of his resources, and he

FAITHFUL UNTO DEATH. 143

suggested that it might be possible to catch shrimps to eke out the very scanty supply of food now available. This suggestion he at once proceeded to put in practice, and having found a suitable place for setting his net, he caught a good supply daily. In fact shrimp soup or stew became thenceforward one of the most important items of the bill of fare.

Notwithstanding the desperate condition of their affairs, even now the men could find time and thought to devote to scientific research. Throughout the whole winter such observations as circumstances would permit were daily made and recorded, and the natural history collections were increased at every opportunity; a little of the precious alcohol being devoted to the preservation of the specimens—one of the many unselfish acts of a band of starving men, among whom unselfishness was the rule rather than the exception.

But for some "the long self-sacrifice of life" was soon to end, for before April was a week old Christiansen and Lynn had passed away. Others were terribly weak. Who would be the next to go was a question that could not fail to arise. For some time Frederick and Rice had been anxious to go in search of the meat abandoned by Elison's party in the previous autumn. As the quantity was comparatively small, Greely at first refused his consent; but when Lynn and Christiansen died of starvation, as the two heroic fellows still wanted to go, he gave them permission to do so. It was decided that they should start on the sixth of April, and as in order to save time they intended to take a short cut across the island to their destination—Baird Inlet—Kislingbury, Brainard, and one or two others took their sledge on in advance. Towards evening Rice and Frederick set out on their desperate errand, and though they frequently stumbled into drifts from which, in their weak and half-starved condition, they had some difficulty in extricating themselves, they managed to travel quickly. At their first camp a storm made it impossible to light their lamp, and with nothing in the way of refreshment but a little frozen pemmican, they betook themselves to their sleeping-bag on the ice. The drifting snow soon covered them, and twenty-two hours passed before the storm allowed them to go on; then hungry and thirsty, but too cold to halt longer, they went on until hard work had so far warmed them that they ventured to stop and cook a meal. The next morning they reached the place which had been originally selected for winter quarters, and as this was within a few miles of the spot where the meat had been abandoned, they left everything except a sledge and a little food, thinking that they would soon be able to find the cache.

Everything, however, was against them. The tide in some places had overflowed the ice, and their shoes thus wetted froze stiff, and the difficulties were increased by another gale with drifting snow, which made it difficult to see where they were going. In the course of the afternoon they reached the spot where according to their reckoning the meat ought to have been; but search as they would, they could find no sign of it, and as Rice was fast becoming knocked up, Frederick suggested that they should return to camp. Rice said that he should soon be all right if they travelled slowly, but in spite of this precaution he seemed to grow worse; so Frederick took matters into his own hands, and insisted on halting while some tea and warm food were cooked, and in the meantime gave Rice a dose of ammonia and rum. But all efforts to restore the stricken man were unavailing: he soon became too weak to stand, and although Frederick took off some of his own clothes in which to wrap him, he rapidly sank; but he never lost consciousness, and up to the time that he died he talked cheerfully to Frederick, who, regardless of cold and snow, sat on the sledge in his shirt sleeves holding his dying comrade. When Rice had passed away, and his services were no longer needed, he too was almost exhausted; but knowing that if he did not return some of the others would come out to look for him, he made his way as best he could to the camp where the things had been left. Food and rest somewhat revived him, and in the morning he tramped back over the floe to the place where the dead man lay, and then having buried him in the snow he turned his face homewards. It was a terrible journey, but at length he accomplished it, marching as far as he could, and then, after taking a spoonful of rum and ammonia, lying down supperless in his bag for a few hours' sleep. On awaking, almost too stiff and cold to move, he again struggled on, until exertion had warmed him, when he stopped, and cooked a little food.

During Frederick's absence death again visited the camp. For some days Lockwood had been failing, and in spite of extra rations of raw dovekie, the only food available, he gradually sank, dying, like the others, calmly and peacefully, and a few days later Jewell too passed away. Living thus face to face with death, Greely's sad words, "To die is easy, very easy; it is only hard to strive, to endure, to live," probably expressed the feelings of all. But "hope springs eternal in the human breast," and when on Easter Sunday morning a snow-bunting was heard chirping outside the hut, every one was cheered and encouraged.

Lockwood's death compelled Greely to desire Kislingbury to return to duty; but in less than a week his mind began to give way, and about the same time Greely's heart became so seriously affected that the doctor considered him in danger of death.

A day or two before Kislingbury broke down, Brainard saw a bear on the ice-foot. As soon as he made known the good news the hunters went off in hot pursuit, and, to the joy of all, they were successful. Four hundred pounds of good meat seemed a godsend, and the men began to hope that after all they might survive until the long-expected succour came.

As time went on the effects of famine showed themselves more and more. The men were affected in different ways: some, like Greely and Israel, though weak and ill physically, were perfectly clear mentally; but the minds of others were thrown completely off their balance, and a few suffered alike in mind and body. Existence had become simply a dreary death-in-life, and as day after day dragged its slow length along, increasing weakness alone marked the passage of time.

Shrimps, fortunately, were fairly plentiful, and Brainard, who seemed to have a knack of catching them, spent a part of every day in attending to the nets—for when anybody else took his place the haul was never a good one. Long and Jens still hunted perseveringly, and having one day found a seal basking in the sun on a detached floe, Jens launched his kayak and went in pursuit. All seemed to be going well, and Long's hopes rose as Jens neared the seal; but suddenly throwing caution to the winds, the Eskimo began to paddle madly. He reached the ice, and tried to spring on to it with his kayak; but as he did so the treacherous floe gave way beneath him, and down he went. Part of the kayak was still visible, and Long made his way as quickly as he could to the spot, though more than once he too was in danger by reason of the ice breaking. But he was too late: the "little man," as Jens was affectionately called, was already dead, having died, as he had lived, in the service of others.

On the twelfth of May the last stores were issued, and thenceforth the party would have to depend solely on shrimps, kelp, saxifrage, and such game as they could procure. The look-out was black indeed; but strangely enough, Pavy, who for weeks had not been in any respect an agreeable member of the party, now worked hard, fetching in a supply of ice for water, and beginning to make a collection of lichen-covered stones. Most of the others, however, were fast losing ground. Private Ellis died on the nineteenth of May, and three days later Ralston breathed his last.

Pavy declared that the dark hut, which the sun's rays seldom reached, was helping to weaken the men; so a tent was pitched in a dry, sunny spot on the hillside, and in the afternoon of the day on which Ralston died the move began. The distance was only a few hundred yards, but it was more than Israel and Whisler could manage. The former collapsed on the way, and had to be put on the sledge; while Whisler became unconscious shortly after his arrival. He died the next day, and within another ten days Israel, Kislingbury, and Salor entered into rest.

Pavy, too, though for a long time he had been one of the strongest of the party, began to fail both physically and mentally; but after a few hours he seemed better, and was able to discuss with Greely the advisability of eating *tripe de roche*. A good deal of this lichen grew in the neighbourhood, but Pavy would not recommend its use, founding his objection on the deleterious effects of the tripe when used by Franklin's expedition. Brainard and others, however, disagreed with the doctor, and in accordance with their wishes the experiment was made. No ill effects followed, and thenceforward the lichen formed part of the daily food of the castaways. The same day Long shot several birds of different kinds; but most of them fell in the water, and he only managed to secure one, which was divided between the hunters, as the only chance of life for all lay in their ability to continue their work.

Sad as had been the experience of the explorers throughout this terrible winter, the worst part was yet to come. Theft after theft of food had been forgiven, but Private Henry, in spite alike of reprimands and promises of amendment, still continued his depredations, though he was by far the strongest of the party. For lack of other food the starving men were now compelled to stew down sealskin thongs and sleeping-bags until the skin was tender enough to eat; but even from this wretched apology for food Henry could not keep his hands, and one or two others were rightly or wrongly suspected. If this continued, all must perish; and in order to secure the greatest good of the greatest number, Greely, having again received undeniable testimony of Henry's dishonesty—indeed he himself admitted his guilt—reluctantly ordered that he should be shot as the only means of saving the lives of the others.

That same day Bender and Dr. Pavy breathed their last. The latter, in his mental aberration, had been dosing himself indiscriminately from the medicine-chest, and some of the drugs which he had taken doubtless hastened his end. Their comrades were now too weak to carry them to the hill-side where the others were buried, and having laid the dead men in a deep crack in the ice, they sadly returned to the tent where several others lay in the extremity of weakness, while, to make matters still worse, Schneider and Connell appeared to be in the early stage of scurvy.

Would no one survive? Unless help came soon it seemed highly probable, for the daily haul of shrimps was now greatly reduced, game was scarce, and Long was almost past hunting. But misfortunes seldom come singly, and on the twelfth of June the ice-floes, which had been broken up by a recent gale, floated off, carrying with them Brainard's shrimp-nets. This was a terrible loss, for it deprived the wretched men of another of their means of support; and still further to depress them, that same evening Sergeant Gardiner died. He had been ill for a long time, and nearly two months before the doctor had said that he would be the next to go; but he had an intense desire to reach home again, and Greely believed that it was

FAITHFUL UNTO DEATH.   151

this, more than anything else, which had kept him alive so long. His death seemed the more sad now that the time had come when it was reasonable to look for the arrival of help. Any day a vessel might come; and as Brainard could do nothing in the way of shrimping until new nets were made, he occupied himself in setting up a flagstaff in a conspicuous position on the rocks.

It was no wonder that the men grew weaker and weaker, especially as they were now reduced to the oil-tanned sealskin sleeping-bags, which even to them were almost uneatable. Schneider now quite broke down, and after a day or two of helplessness, he died on the evening of the eighteenth of June. Three or four days later only one or two still had strength to move. Bierderbick was almost crippled by rheumatism; Greely and Connell were too weak to stand; Elison was absolutely helpless; and Frederick, Brainard, and Long were barely able to crawl. But "when the night is darkest dawn is nearest," and when things seemed at the worst a distant noise was heard. It sounded like the whistle of a steamer, and though Greely could hardly believe that it could be so, he asked Brainard and Long to go to the hill and look out. They did so, but in a few minutes came back saying that there was nothing in sight. There was nothing that they could do, and Brainard lay down again, to wait for the death which could not be far off.

In a few minutes voices were heard. The long

waiting was over, for relief had come at last. Had it been delayed an hour or two longer, it would have been too late to save Connell, who was almost at his last gasp. A spoonful or two of whisky still remained, and faithful, unselfish Bierderbick, as soon as he heard the voices of the rescue-party, poured a spoonful down Connell's throat. He wished to give the remainder to Greely, who was hardly less exhausted; but when the lieutenant, with noble self-forgetfulness, refused to drink, it too was given to Connell.

Once on board the ship the troubles of the explorers were at an end, though, much to their disgust, it was a long time before they were allowed to eat and drink as much as they chose. They all arrived safely at Godhavn, where Elison died from the effects of an operation on his frozen limbs. Poor fellow! he had suffered much, and it seemed hard that no better fate awaited him, although to a man of his stamp death may have been preferable to living as a cripple. The rest of the party arrived safely at home, and America and England united in congratulating the men who, having surpassed all previous Arctic explorers, had crowned noble work by yet nobler endurance of untold suffering.

CHAPTER XVII.

DEAD YET SPEAKING.

A COUPLE of years before Greely set out on his ill-fated expedition, Lieutenant George Washington de Long sailed in command of the *Jeannette* from San Francisco in the hope of reaching the long-sought North Pole *viâ* Behring Strait. Up to that time very little had been done in the way of Polar exploration by this route, and the popular notions of the geography, or rather oceanography, of the eastern half of the North Polar basin were in consequence remarkably vague. Some scientists believed that Wrangel Land was an extension of Greenland, and that a well-found expedition with plenty of dogs might manage to travel indefinitely along its shores, possibly to the Pole itself, and then on westward down the Greenland coast. This plan was suggested to Mr. James Gordon Bennett, the wealthy proprietor of *The New York Herald;* and after spending much time in looking for a suitable ship, he purchased Sir Allen Young's Arctic yacht *Pandora*, rechristened her *Jeannette,* and then having had her thoroughly overhauled and strengthened, he gave the command to De Long.

The expedition sailed on July 8, 1879. Almost from the outset luck was against the *Jeannette*. Less than two months after she left San Francisco she was caught in the ice, and in a few days was frozen in so firmly that escape was evidently hopeless. From that time forward the cruel floes never relaxed their grip; but they were not stationary, and she was carried north-westward past Wrangel Land, exploding effectually all theories respecting its continental nature. Thus month after month passed. Sometimes the ice drifted south or south-east—of course carrying the *Jeannette* with it—but more often it took her in a north-westerly direction. At last the northern drift became so decided that De Long and his comrades began to hope that they would eventually reach— somewhere, possibly the Pole itself.

These hopes were, however, destined to disappointment. Twenty-one months after, the *Jeannette* was frozen in; and when she had reached about 77° 15′ north latitude, a terrible nip occurred, and the luckless ship, crushed like an egg-shell, went down so quickly that her crew had barely time to carry their boats and stores to a safe position on the ice. After almost incredible difficulties, they made their way in safety to the New Siberian Islands, whence they essayed to reach the mainland, but on the way a storm arose which separated the boats. One probably went down in the gale, for no trace of it or its crew could afterwards be found; but the other two, commanded respectively by De Long and Engineer Melville, landed safely in different parts of the Lena Delta. Of the two parties Melville's was the more fortunate, for they soon fell in with natives, by whose help they eventually reached civilization. De Long and his companions having meanwhile passed through terrible hardships, made their way to land at a point north-west of the spot where Melville landed, and then, misled by incorrect charts, they struggled on through the pathless snows of the delta, until, like Franklin's men, "they fell down and died as they walked along." Of this boat's crew two men only— Noros and Nindemann—escaped by the skin of their teeth, and after passing through much tribulation, were rescued by Melville, who had been informed of their whereabouts by natives and Russian exiles and officials.

But though De Long was dead and his ship lay at the bottom of the Arctic Ocean, the expedition, which seemed to be a failure, was the means of solving the Arctic problem. When the retreat from the *Jeannette* began, sundry odds and ends were left on the ice, and these were supposed to have disappeared, like the ship herself, from mortal ken. But not so. Three years passed, and then, far away from the scene of the wreck, some of the lost articles were found on an ice-floe near Julianshaab in south-west Greenland. There was no mistaking them: a pair of linen trousers marked "Louis Noros," a list of provisions written and signed by De Long, and a manuscript list of the *Jeannette's* boats could have emanated from nowhere but the *Jeannette*.

The matter eventually came to the knowledge of Fridtjof Nansen, a young Norwegian scientist, and at once set him thinking. How on earth had the things reached Julianshaab? Of this riddle there was but one solution. The current which had been carrying the *Jeannette* herself northward had continued to carry the floe bearing the derelict articles, and after carrying it right across the Polar basin and down the east coast of Greenland, took it round Cape Farewell and on up the west coast towards Davis Strait. The more Nansen thought the more clear did it become that a strong current must sweep from east to west across the Polar basin. But good work is seldom done in a hurry, and biding his time he patiently collected evidence in support of his theory.

Further testimony was obtained on his memorable journey across the inland ice of Greenland in 1888. Before he and his companions effected a landing, they drifted for many days among the pack on the east coast of that inhospitable land; but Nansen turned even this time to account, and whenever he got the chance collected dust and mud from the floes which in company with his own boat were rapidly drifting southward, impelled by a strong current. The dust then gathered was afterwards sent to the Swedish geologist Törnebohm, who, having microscopically examined it, found that it consisted of about twenty different varieties of minerals. He knew nothing of Nansen's views respecting the supposed current, but so great was the variety that he thought the dust must originally have come from North Siberia.

Other samples of dust from the same floes were examined by Professor Cleve of Upsala, whose specialty was the study of diatoms. He found the dust different from anything else which he had ever examined, except one sample which was submitted to him by a member of Nordenskiöld's party who had collected it on the ice near Behring Strait. Further, some years before, an Eskimo "throwing-stick" of a peculiar make used by the natives of Alaska, and by no other Eskimos, was found near Godthaab.

All these finds of course strengthened Nansen's theory. In fact, they practically confirmed it; for how was it possible that diatoms and throwing-sticks from the shores of Behring Strait, not to mention mineral dust and driftwood from Northern Siberia, could by any means have found their way to the shores of Greenland, unless carried thither by some powerful current which swept across the Polar basin? Thought with Nansen generally led to action. That such a current existed he had no doubt whatever; and why, he argued, should not a current which could carry icefloes be pressed into the service of science, and made to carry a ship? Many explorers had tried to reach the Pole *viâ* Smith Sound and Robeson Channel, but hitherto all attempts had failed, mainly, as Nansen thought, because the explorers were fighting against nature instead of working with her. Probably, as in the case of the celebrated tub owned by the wise men of Gotham,

> "Had the *Jeannette* been stronger,
> Her story had been longer;"

and instead of going to the bottom when nipped by the ice, she would have accomplished the feat actually performed by the various articles abandoned by her crew, and in due time have drifted across the Polar area, finally arriving triumphantly in open water somewhere between Greenland and Spitzbergen.

Under these circumstances, the proper course was evidently to build a ship strong enough to withstand the ice pressure. This Nansen believed he could do, and it would then only remain to provision her carefully with the very best preserved meats, vegetables, and bread available, and to man her with a crew of hardy fellows, who in the cause of geographical discovery would "dare do all that might become a man."

Unfortunately the scheme, like most other new ideas, met with opposition even in scientific quarters. Greely called it "Dr. Nansen's illogical scheme of self-destruction," and Nares found it extremely difficult to believe that any ship built by human hands could withstand a genuine Polar nip, but in spite of his doubts he wished well to the voyage. Sir Allen Young, however, was more hopeful, and a good many people thought that, supposing the scheme to be any way practicable, Nansen was the man to make it succeed. His own countrymen at any rate believed in him. His Greenland journey had convinced them of his powers, and though, when he applied for a grant on that occasion, government declined to have anything to do with the matter, the Storthing now voted a grant of 200,000 kroner towards the equipment of the expedition. Nor were private subscriptions lacking. The Royal Geographical Society of England subscribed £300, and donations poured in, not only from Norway and England, but from many friends and well-wishers in other countries. The undertaking might fairly be called an international one; and thus provided with the sinews of war, it only remained for Nansen to go forward and prosper. With that object before him he called his ship *Fram*, the Norwegian equivalent for " forward."

Preparations, of course, took some time. The *Fram* was specially constructed from Nansen's own designs. Not only was she the strongest ship, probably, that was ever turned out of a dockyard, but her hull was pointed at both ends, and was rounded in such a manner that there was nothing for the ice to take hold of; and should it close upon her, she would of necessity, instead of being crushed, rise with the pressure. Even the keel scarcely offered any projection and she was altogether, as Nansen said, "round and slippery like an eel."

She was not very big: for size does not necessarily imply strength; indeed in Arctic vessels size is very apt to detract from strength, and a large ship is less easily handled in the ice than a small one. Consequently the *Fram* was merely of sufficient size to accommodate about a dozen men, and to carry fuel and stores sufficient on a liberal computation for about six years. Her construction and equipment came rather expensive; but Nansen did not believe in stinting when so much was at stake, and he would have nothing that was not the very best of its kind. No provisions were accepted until a sample had been carefully analyzed, and he took advantage of all the modern improvements in the preparation of tinned and preserved foods, to secure for his men almost as great a variety of eatables as they could have had on shore.

Nor was the scientific aspect of the expedition in any way overlooked. Nansen's object was not so much to reach the Pole itself as to cross the Polar basin, and make scientific observations, take soundings, and, in fact, learn all he could about that hitherto unexplored ocean. With this end in view, he supplied himself with a large assortment of scientific instruments of the best make; and when all preparations of this kind were finished, he had merely

THE LAUNCH OF THE "FRAM." *Page 159.*

THE "FRAM" GETTING READY TO SAIL. *Page 160.*

DEAD YET SPEAKING.

to select his crew. First and foremost came Otto Sverdrup, one of Nansen's companions on his Greenland journey. He was a first-rate sailor, and knew nearly as much about ice as Nansen himself—in fact there was very little that Sverdrup could not do, and he was, in consequence, appointed captain of the *Fram*. Next came Lieutenant Sigurd Scott-Hansen, who filled the post of meteorologist and astronomer; while Dr. Henrick Blessing, the surgeon, undertook also the duties of botanist—a task not likely to be a very arduous one among Arctic ice. The mate was Theodore Jacobsen, who had an extensive acquaintance with ice; and Anton Amundsen took charge of the engineering department, in which he was ably seconded by Bernhard Nordahl, who also added to his duties the care of the dynamo which supplied electric light to the ship. Lars Pettersen shipped as smith and machinist, but he afterwards took over the duties of cook—a post originally held by Adolph Juell, who for the purposes of this voyage renounced his proper standing of ship's captain. The ship's company also included Lieutenant F. Hjalmar Johansen, who, rather than stay behind, accepted the post of stoker; Peter Henriksen, harpooner to the expedition; and Ivor Mogstad, carpenter.

As it was on the cards that a great deal of work might have to be done by sledges, a team of dogs was a most desirable addition to the equipment. Sledge-dogs, however, could not be procured in

Europe, and Nansen arranged with Baron von Toll, a celebrated Siberian explorer, that a strong team should await the arrival of the *Fram* at Khabarova, a Samoyede settlement on Yugor Strait, where he also hoped to complete his stock of coal. By the middle of June 1893 all was in order, and on midsummer day the *Fram* sailed from Christiania under the charge of Scott-Hansen, who navigated her as far as Trondhjem, where Sverdrup came on board and took command.

In due time the *Fram* arrived at Tromsö, where she took in as much coal as she could conveniently carry, as well as a supply of sundry articles not obtainable in lower latitudes. These included reindeer-meat, fur clothing; "komager," a kind of moccasin peculiar to the Lapps; and "finnesko," or Finn shoes, which, when well stuffed with dry grass, have the reputation of being exceedingly desirable foot-gear for snowy countries. The ship's company, too, was augmented by the addition to its number of Bernt Bentzen, a jolly, good-tempered sailor, who, having come to see Nansen about an hour before the *Fram* sailed, was so well pleased with the ship and her crew that he stayed on board for good.

The last calling-place in Europe was Vardö, at the mouth of Varanger Fiord. Vardö is a place of microscopic dimensions; but its inhabitants made up for their lack of number by their enthusiasm, and a grand reception and sumptuous banquet were ac-

TROMSÖ. *Page 162.*

corded to the explorers, who, above all others at that time, were the men whom Norway delighted to honour.

A good deal of ice was encountered in Barents Sea; but much to Nansen's delight, the *Fram* proved herself worthy of her name, and pushed forward through the pack as if ice-floes were obstacles of no moment whatever. Nansen himself navigated her from an exalted position in the crow's-nest, and it was with no small joy that he watched his ship insinuate herself into the ice, breaking it up and pushing it aside with the utmost ease, while at the same time she was as handy and manageable as a small boat. With such a ship, in spite of fog and ice, a quick passage was made, and on the evening of the twenty-ninth of July, a red flag floating from a tall flagstaff on the shore indicated that Khabarova was not far distant. The dilapidated hulls of a couple of wrecked vessels warned the travellers to approach with caution; but the shoals were safely passed, and the *Fram* dropped anchor in full view of the somewhat uninteresting settlement. The place consisted mainly of Samoyede tents, though here and there the scene was varied by a house inhabited probably by one of the Russian merchants who visit Khabarova during the summer to trade with the natives, whom they supply with brandy and other European commodities in exchange for the furs and oil which are the staple products of the locality.

Hardly was the ship in harbour when a boat put off from the shore, and in a little while a man came on board. He did not look much like a Samoyede, and soon proved not to be one, but the man whom at the moment Nansen most desired to see—namely, the custodian of the dogs. His name was Trontheim, and he soon set the explorers' minds at rest by telling them he had got five-and-thirty Ostiak dogs, as fine animals as they could wish to see, awaiting their arrival. He did his charges no more than justice, and the travellers were delighted with the gentle-looking, handsome dogs—some snow-white and long-coated, with pointed ears and muzzles; some shorter haired, bushy-tailed, and fox-like; others black or spotted. But amiable as they looked, they delighted "to bark and bite" when occasion arose, and one day when they fell furiously upon an unlucky Samoyede dog who incautiously crossed their path, it was all that Nansen and Trontheim could do to save that hapless animal from being reduced to a fragmentary condition.

While waiting for the arrival of the promised coal, Nansen and Sverdrup went in the petroleum-launch to inspect the state of the ice in the Kara Sea. This seemed promising enough; but Yugor Strait was far too shallow for safe navigation, and in returning the launch broke her propeller by a collision with an unseen stone. This made the return to the ship a work of time, and necessitated several hours of hard work for Nansen and Amundsen before the launch was again fit for service.

The coal did not come—probably the ice in Barents Sea had delayed the vessel which was to bring it; and having waited as long as he dared, Nansen took the dogs on board and sailed without the coal. To do so was annoying; but, after all, it did not really matter, for the *Fram* had already a good stock of fuel on board, and a further supply was desirable merely as an additional precaution against a possible deten- in the ice beyond the time originally contemplated.

CHAPTER XVIII.

FIRE AND ICE.

ON the fourth of August the anchor was hauled up, but before the *Fram* was fairly under way a thick fog came on. This seemed, indeed, to be a frequent condition of the atmosphere in that neighbourhood; and as the mist showed no signs of taking its departure, Nansen considered that to wait for it to do so would be only a waste of time. The recent accident to the launch had, however, fully impressed him with the dangers attendant on the navigation of Yugor Strait, and not being minded to risk running the ship aground, with Scott-Hansen as his companion he led the way in the launch. From time to time the engine required a fresh supply of petroleum, and once while Nansen, who acted as stoker, was attending to its needs, an unexpected jerk caused him to spill a little oil; this at once caught fire, and ran blazing along the bottom of the boat, where sundry pools of previously spilt oil quickly added to the conflagration.

Nansen's clothes also had been liberally bedewed

FIRE AND ICE.

with petroleum, and being in consequence in a highly inflammable state, speedily caught fire, while a bucket full of petroleum which stood near added its quota to the general blaze. The fire threatened to become serious; but there was plenty of water at hand, and Nansen was not the man to stand still and allow either himself or his boat to be burnt. He soon extinguished his own clothes, and then, having consigned the flaming oil-bucket to a suitable resting-place in the sea, he poured water over the boat until the conflagration was finally subdued. The rest of the strait was safely navigated. But in the Kara Sea things went less smoothly—

> "The ice was here, the ice was there,
> The ice was all around,"

and with the obstructiveness natural to ice, did its best to bar further progress; but it fortunately overlooked a narrow channel near the shore, and through this the gallant little ship threaded her way, until off the Yalmal Peninsula the pack closed in. Near the coast the water was very shallow—so shallow, in fact, that when some of the party went ashore they were obliged, when still some distance from the beach, to get out of the boat and wade.

When they were at last fairly ashore, they found little to reward them for their trouble in getting there. On every side dreary, flat, barren, treeless tundras stretched away as far as the eye could reach;

not that this was very far, for, as usual, fog obscured the view. The few pieces of driftwood on the beach were sunk deep in the wet sand, and with the exception of a snipe or two, and here and there a few flowers, not a sign of life was to be seen. But desolate as the place was, it had its inhabitants; for a couple of Samoyedes came off to the *Fram*, where, much to their joy, they were presented with some biscuits and other European commodities.

In due time the ice relented, and allowed the explorers to proceed; but on reaching the extremity of the Yalmal Peninsula, a strong wind blowing steadily from the north-east brought up a heavy sea, against which the much-enduring *Fram* had to make her way as best she could. While thus toiling along the coast, an island hitherto uncharted was discovered, which, in compliment to Sverdrup, who first espied it, was named Sverdrup's Island. This was the first of many new islands discovered off the Siberian coast: in some parts they lay so thick that it was no easy matter to keep note of them. Near Taimyr Island the ice lay in a dense, impenetrable pack, and the ship was headed southward, but nowhere was an open channel to be found; everything was hermetically sealed by ice too thick for even the *Fram* to tackle, and all she could do was to coast along its edge. While thus engaged the curious phenomenon of dead water was seen. A layer of fresh water overspread the salt water, and as the ship moved,

FIRE AND ICE. 169

glided along with it. The two kinds of water kept themselves quite distinct: that at the top was sweet enough to drink, while the genuine sea-water below was too strongly impregnated with salt for use even in the boiler.

At last the ice proved altogether too much for the *Fram*, and she was moored to the edge of the floe to await better times; but an accommodating storm broke up the ice, and allowed her to continue her course. Cape Chelyuskin was in due time safely reached, and the occasion was celebrated by a bowl of punch—an unusual luxury on board the *Fram*. But again the ice caused delay, and hardly was the cape rounded when the pack forced the explorers to anchor. Not to waste any time, an inland excursion was undertaken, the principal result of which was the discovery of a hitherto unknown inlet of considerable extent. After this, for several days the *Fram* made her way through more islands and more ice, the pack being in many places so thick that it was impossible to make much progress.

One day several walruses were seen lying on a floe not very far from the ship. The opportunity was too tempting to be lost, so in hot haste harpoons were sharpened, guns and cartridges prepared, and Henriksen, Nansen, and Juell tumbled into a boat and pulled off.

Advancing cautiously, they reached the floe where the intended victims were unsuspiciously basking in the sun, and Henriksen, as soon as the boat was within convenient range, let fly his harpoon. Unfortunately his aim was not perfect, and the harpoon merely glided over the animals, who promptly rose up, and bellowing loudly came over to the edge of the ice near the boat. This suited Nansen very well; he fired, and one of the biggest of the monsters fell into the water. Another shot had a like effect; but by this time the herd was thoroughly alarmed by the noise of the guns and the unaccountable behaviour of their companions. One after another the huge brutes dashed into the water, and in a minute or two they crowded round the boat, roaring and bellowing—diving here, rising there—and churning up the water into a mass of foam. The commotion became rather alarming. It would have been an easy matter for the walruses, had they been so minded, to capsize the boat, and a blow or two from their tusks would have sent her to the bottom like a stone; but no disaster happened, and finally a couple of walruses were secured. A third was shot; but Henriksen had used up his harpoons, and having no means of securing the huge carcass, it sank before the *Fram* reached the scene of conflict.

Two or three days after this encounter the *Fram* arrived off the mouth of the Olenek River, where it had been arranged that a further supply of dogs, reputed better even than those shipped at Khabarova, should await the coming of the explorers. It was

WALRUS. Page 170.

most desirable to have these dogs; but the season was getting late, delays had already been too numerous, and shallow water near the mouth of the river suggested the possibility of a further detention of indefinite duration should the vessel run aground. Even a few days' delay might have serious consequences, for it was not likely that navigation would remain open much longer, and to be ice-bound on the Siberian coast would have accorded ill with Nansen's plans and wishes. On the whole, therefore, it seemed wiser to be content with the dogs already on board than to risk getting the ship aground; so, leaving this dangerous locality, the explorers steered for the New Siberian Islands.

Everything looked most encouraging, and the *Fram* steamed merrily on through open water of apparently unlimited extent. Sverdrup, who was perhaps more hopeful than any one, had visions of wonderful latitudes to be attained if only—and it was a big "if"—this state of things would continue for a few days. But circumstances were not propitious. Five days after leaving the Olenek an impervious ice-pack blocked the way, and though the fog, to the presence of which the explorers were by this time pretty well accustomed, shut out any distant view, the obstruction appeared to extend for miles both eastward and westward. Which way would it be most desirable to go? To the northward progress was impossible, and as the edge of the pack to the eastward seemed to trend in a southerly direction, it was decided that an attempt should be made to advance westward. For a few hours the *Fram* steamed on, but then, for the very sufficient reason that she had entered a bay in the ice from which she could only emerge by doubling back on her route, she was anchored to the edge of a floe to await further developments. The position, on the whole, was not a bad one. It would, of course, have been pleasant to advance further before being frozen in; but if this was not to be, it would not have been an easy matter to better the *Fram's* position: so no further attempt was made to extricate her from the ice, and in a few days she was firmly frozen in.

Every one now busied himself with preparations for winter. First of all the boilers were cleaned, the machinery was oiled, the rudder hauled up, and the coal moved to a more convenient position than that which it had hitherto occupied. Everything, in fact, was put in order; for the *Fram* had now practically abandoned her nautical character, and had begun a new stage of her career as an Arctic residence. Various workshops were fitted up: the hold was transformed into a carpenter's shop, the engine-room into machine-works, and a blacksmith's shop was established on deck; even the saloon did not long remain exempt, for shoemaking and other work of a more or less domestic character was carried on within its walls.

The equinox was long past. Daily the sun sank lower, and the lengthening nights warned the ship's company that they would do well to get the electric light into working order. Somebody had suggested that the dynamo should be worked by wind-power, so a windmill was erected, and supplied with sails so large that a very slight breeze would keep them in motion. In due time all these preparations were carried out, but even then there seemed to be little chance of anybody having much idle time. There was always something to be done in one or other of the workshops, in the galley or some other domestic department; and in addition to these useful but prosaic occupations, several of the party had their time pretty well filled with scientific work. The doctor had less to do in his own line than anybody on board, for the whole company, with a beautiful unanimity, refused to fall ill. Blessing, in consequence, had nothing to do except to study, and note the effects of Arctic cold and darkness on European constitutions.

Long before the preparations for winter were completed, the *Fram* was firmly embedded in her icy cradle, and had begun to drift with the pack in a northerly direction. This was what everybody wanted, and for that reason, perhaps, the wind changed its direction, and drove ice and ship southwards. Week after week this contrary drift continued, until by the eighth of November the ship had reached 77° 43′ north latitude—rather further south than she had been when she met with the ice on the twentieth of September. Then at last the wind became more accommodating: it went round to the south, and throughout the winter the *Fram* moved towards the Pole, just as Nansen had supposed would be the case. The ice, however, was by no means placid, and the floes crushed and ground together in a manner which, to most ships in the *Fram's* position, would have been highly detrimental, but to all the commotion Nansen's ship remained calmly indifferent. Closer and closer the ice pressed around her; louder and louder grew the many noises—the cracks, the groans and grumbles, the snarls and roars, like the voices of tortured giants—that added to the hideousness of the ice-conflict; but in spite of it all the *Fram* behaved as her designer and builder had expected. Her smooth, rounded hull offered no projection for the ice to grip; and as it pressed around her, she simply rose as though she were being gently borne up by a lever, until the ice broke beneath her, and she glided back into her original position.

Here was a triumph indeed; and as his theories resolved themselves into accomplished facts, Nansen's spirits rose, and his fears, if he had ever had any, took wing and departed. At first he and his companions had watched the ice with some anxiety; but finding that not one of the *Fram's* timbers started or even cracked, they soon lost interest in the ice-battle outside their fortress, though the thunder of the contending forces rose sometimes to such a pitch that ordinary conversation was drowned in the tumult.

As it became clear that the *Fram* was really frozen in, and that her next appearance in the character of a ship need not be expected to take place for many months—possibly years—to come, her crew settled down to Arctic life. They generally rose about eight, and after a genuine Norwegian breakfast—meat, cheese, tongue, fish, porridge, bread or biscuits, marmalade, etc.—they dispersed to attend to their various duties. At one o'clock all hands assembled for dinner, and then, after taking their ease for an hour or so, those who had still anything to do resumed their occupations, and continued until six o'clock, when supper was served and the duties of the day ended.

Occasionally a little sport broke in on the monotony of life. One day when Scott-Hansen and one or two others were setting up an observatory tent on the ice, a bear came up, intending probably to offer his assistance. But his services were not desired, and as soon as he appeared on the scene, the proprietors of the tent, being unprepared for his visit, hurriedly made tracks for the ship. Meanwhile Nansen turned out with his rifle and the dogs, and gave the visitor such a warm reception that, when stripped of his warm white coat and transferred to the larder, he offered no remonstrance whatever. Not that the dogs had much to do with the matter, for—softly be it spoken—they showed no desire whatever to improve their acquaintance with this their first Polar bear.

During the voyage from Khabarova, and for some days after the ship was frozen in, they were kept tied up; but as the cold increased they required more exercise, and were allowed to be at liberty during the day. Had they been more peaceably disposed, the plan would doubtless have worked well; but as it was, fights were of frequent occurrence, and more than one dog came to an untimely end when feeling in canine circles ran unusually high. "Might is right" seemed to be a generally-accepted axiom, and acting on this the whole pack would set on any dog who got worsted in fair fight, and give him a very rough time—so much so that one or two timid bow-wows hardly dared to venture off the ship.

As time went on several bears made their appearance, and the dogs began to take a healthy interest in their visits. One night a tremendous barking was heard on the floe—not that noise among the dogs was by any means an unusual occurrence, but this time the commotion was so great that it aroused Scott-Hansen's curiosity, and he went to see what in the world could be the matter. In a short time he returned, saying that he had seen something—what he did not know, but it was too big to be a dog. Of course the sportsmen turned out, and after a little rifle practice at the big intruder, they went down on to the ice. The result of their shooting was most satisfactory. There lay a dead bear with two bullet-holes in his coat, and further inspection showed that

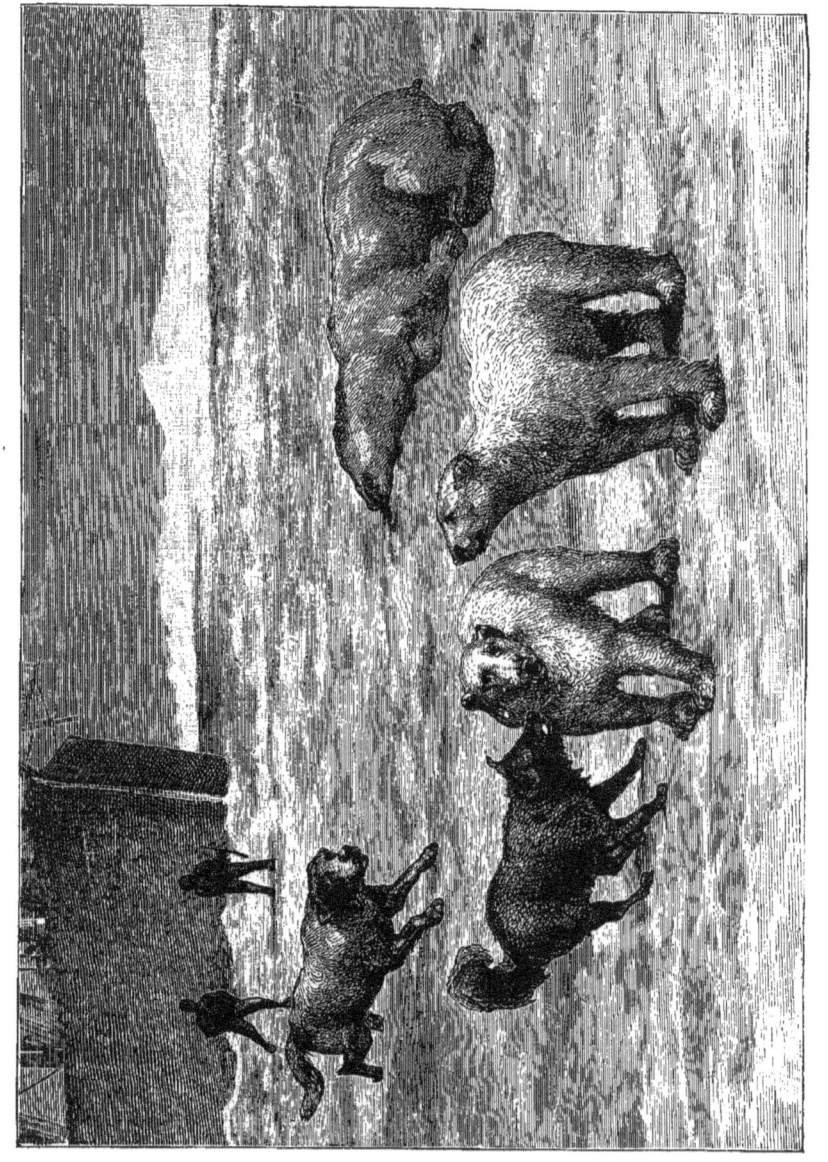

he had been accompanied by a second bear, who, to judge by his track, had been severely wounded. In the morning the trail was followed, and at no great distance from the ship the injured bear was seen making his way over the ice as well as his disabled condition would allow. Like most Arctic animals, he had a remarkable power of endurance, or he could hardly have travelled so far, for he had been shot through the back in such a way that he had no power whatever in his hind legs. But in spite of his injuries he contrived to reach a water-pool. Into this he dived, to the great excitement of the dogs, who rushed barking round and round the hole, into which, if they had been allowed to have their own way, they would in their excitement have jumped. A rope was procured, and as soon as a favourable opportunity occurred it was slipped over the bear's paw, hauled tight, and somebody having sent a bullet into the animal's head, the capture was completed.

These nocturnal visits showed Nansen that it was not wise to leave the dogs at large at night, so, with a view to their greater safety, they were brought on board in the evening. The precaution, however, did not always effect its purpose. Late one evening when all the crew were below, such a hubbub arose on deck that Nansen and several others went up to see what was going on. Evidently the dogs had found something to interest them, for they were barking furiously at the side, and though nothing was to be seen, the men concluded that a bear must be somewhere not far off. They were not in want of fresh meat, and the dogs being on deck were supposed to be quite safe; so, as it was considerably warmer in the saloon, the men soon went below again.

The noise, however, continued. It seemed as if heavy weights were being dragged about, and Henriksen, who went up to ascertain the cause, found that three dogs were missing. He supposed they had gone off on their own account, but thinking they would soon return, he did not trouble himself further about the matter until the morning, when he and Mogstad on going to feed and loose the dogs found that the missing trio had not come back. This would not do, and taking a lantern the two men went in search. They had not gone far when the barking and yelping recommenced, and a bear, with the dogs in full cry behind him, ran towards them. Being unarmed, the wisdom of retreating became evident, and Mogstad, who was the fleeter of foot, quickly reached the *Fram* and scrambled on board, where he caused some commotion by shouting for a gun.

Henriksen, meanwhile, in his headlong flight had got entangled among the hummocks; and as he was wearing stiff, wooden-soled shoes, peculiarly ill adapted for rapid locomotion on the ice, he soon measured his length, which was considerable. But he was soon on his feet again, and lantern in hand reached the ship in safety. But just as he got alongside something ranged up towards him. In the uncertain light he thought it was a big dog, but a heavy growl and a sharp bite in the side soon undeceived him, and in the absence of any better means of defence, he dashed the lighted lantern full into the bear's face. Such conduct was quite unexpected by Bruin, and in his surprise and disgust he let go of his assailant, who, throwing away the shattered lantern, scrambled on board in very undignified haste, while the bear endeavoured to soothe his ruffled feelings at the expense of an unlucky dog, who got badly chawed for his lack of caution in venturing within reach.

By this time several of the party were hanging over the ship's side with their rifles, but that morning everything went wrong. One rifle, greased "not wisely but too well," was frozen and unmanageable, another was minus cartridges, from a third the plug had not been removed, and thus some seconds passed before the intruder was finally disposed of. Having got rid of the enemy—a mere cub—a search was instituted, and at a little distance from the ship the mangled carcasses of two dogs were found. Apparently the bear had been on board more than once, and each time had carried off a dog. The third dog was still unaccounted for; but early the following morning Johansen thought he heard a distant howling, and an hour or two later, when Henriksen went to give the dogs their breakfast, the wanderer was standing on the ice alongside.

Notwithstanding intense cold, long-continued darkness, and the unavoidable monotony of life on an ice-bound ship, the crew of the *Fram* found their time pass happily. They seemed, indeed, to be specially constructed for Arctic service, since with a temperature of $-22°$ or so a fire in the saloon was found to be unnecessary, and Bentzen would calmly go on deck in his shirt sleeves to read the thermometer when it indicated a like absence of heat. Wolfskin clothing had been provided, but these cold-loving mortals voted it too warm; and even when the thermometer fell to $-40°$, they still declared that it was not cold enough to wear wolfskin if there was any hard work to be done. They preferred woollen clothing, over which suits of thin, closely-woven canvas were worn as a protection against wind and drifting snow.

CHAPTER XIX.

STILL DRIFTING.

SLOWLY the winter night dragged its length along; but whatever gloom there might be outside, no one was willing to admit it as a guest on board the *Fram*, and Christmas, the chief festival of the year to Norwegians, was kept with general rejoicing. Work was laid aside, the saloon was decorated, the cook surpassed himself in the excellence of the cakes and other delicacies, of which he provided an abundant supply, and presents were distributed to everybody. Of these, several boxes had been sent in advance by friends at home, and the kindly thought added not a little to the pleasure of the recipients, shut out as they were from all intercourse with the outer world.

About the middle of January a dim twilight began to give evidence that the sun was still somewhere in the sky. At first, it is true, the light was very faint; but it increased daily, and by the end of the month a newspaper could be read out of doors. Everything was going well, even the drift was satisfactory, and on the second of February the announcement that the eightieth parallel of north latitude had been passed was received with general satisfaction. The conduct of the *Fram* herself was all that could be desired; for though the ice made sundry attempts to crush her, she treated them with silent contempt, merely rising in her bed as the floes closed upon her.

Up to this time the Polar Sea had been supposed to be a shallow basin, but when the return of daylight allowed of soundings being taken, the depth of the water was found to be far in excess of anything hitherto imagined. None of the sounding-lines provided were long enough to reach the bottom, but a spare steel cable having been pulled to pieces, was ingeniously worked into a new line. This answered well, and depths varying from 1,800 to 2,100 fathoms were recorded: the lowest sea temperature—29·3°—was obtained between twenty-one and forty-three fathoms from the surface. Taking these observations was far from being an unmixed joy, for the instruments seized every opportunity of becoming clogged with ice, and thus retarding the work.

The approach of summer was the signal for the appearance of various sea-birds, among them several specimens of Ross's gull, which, as this bird is one of the rarest of the feathered tribe, were promptly shot, and added to Nansen's collection. Curiously enough, though in the depth of winter more than one bear had been shot, during the spring and most of the summer none came near the ship, and August was far advanced before a chance occurred of replenishing the stock of bear-meat. But the opportunity, when at last it came, was not neglected. Blessing and Johansen turned out with their revolvers—the first weapons that came to hand—and patiently waited until Bruin, unsuspicious of danger, came within convenient range, when both fired together, with the result that roast bear formed a prominent item in that day's bill of fare.

So far as the drift was concerned, things were not now going quite as well as could be wished. During the summer and early autumn the ice—and, of course, the ship with it—was carried in a south-easterly direction; but as winter approached matters righted themselves, and once more the *Fram* pursued her northward way.

Nansen, however, was not fully satisfied. Even in the summer it was clear to him that, in spite of an occasional southerly drift, the *Fram* would eventually be carried across the Polar basin, and judging by the course she was taking, he thought it probable that she would be carried past the north coast of Franz Josef Land. But could he not improve upon this? There was so much westing in her drift that it was obvious she would not touch the Pole, and little by little a new plan began to take shape in Nansen's mind.

It was a daring project, and one that very few would venture even to contemplate. As already stated, Nansen's whole plan was characterized by General Greely as "an illogical scheme of self-destruction." What, then, would have been his opinion of a further development which involved travelling northward with one companion, a dog-team, and a limited supply of provisions across the drifting pack to the Pole, and then getting home without rejoining the ship? Even to Nansen himself the idea when it first arose was startling, but once admitted to his mind it refused to depart, and the more he thought the less impracticable did the venture appear.

For some time he said nothing, but quietly turned over the *pros* and *cons*, thought of difficulties, and considered possibilities, but still the idea strengthened until it became a fixed purpose. The daring schemer then took Sverdrup into his confidence, and the two fully discussed the matter and arranged a definite plan.

It was manifest that the spring would be the proper season for such an undertaking; but though in another eighteen months the ship would doubtless have been carried much nearer to the Pole, she would also have drifted a long way to the westward—too far, Nansen thought, to suit his purpose. True, he had no intention of attempting to return to the ship; that would be, on the face of it, an impossibility, seeing that the rate and direction of her drift during his absence would be unknown to him. He intended,

STILL DRIFTING. 185

therefore, having reached the Pole—or if that proved impracticable, the highest latitude attainable—to steer as straight a course as he could for Franz Josef Land or Spitzbergen, whichever of them seemed the easier of access. Too much westing would upset calculations altogether. So it was decided that the trip should be made in the ensuing spring.

For the accomplishment of the journey Nansen relied mainly on the dogs; but here arose a difficulty —how were they to be fed? To take a full supply of food for them would be impossible, as the sledge-loads must necessarily be of very limited weight; but Nansen proposed to kill some of the dogs to feed the others. Once ashore on either Franz Josef Land or Spitzbergen he had no doubt that game in plenty—bears, seals, or walruses—would be available, and there would then be no further difficulty in supplying both the human and canine explorers with as much food as they required.

Of course Nansen did not attempt to hide from himself that difficulties and dangers, such, for instance, as had befallen Markham, might again arise. Well, if they did, they must; but as far as Nansen could see, there was no reason why the ice nearer to the Pole should be materially worse than in the neighbourhood of the *Fram*. As for scurvy, certainly the Nares Expedition had suffered terribly; but others had escaped, and with the excellent provisions carried by the *Fram*, there was every reason to hope that this danger was infinitesimal. At any rate, though "'tis not in mortals to command success," such mortals as Nansen know how to deserve it, and he was fully determined to do his best.

But before spring and its adventures could arrive, there was another long winter to be faced; and as it approached, the crew of the *Fram* took in hand sundry alterations likely to add to their comfort. Hitherto petroleum had been burnt in the cooker; but as it was important that there should be an abundant supply of this oil for lighting purposes, Nansen contrived a new apparatus to burn coal-oil, of which there was a large quantity on board. The first time the new fuel was tried an explosion took place, with the result that the walls of the galley, as well as the cook's face, were plentifully besprinkled with smuts; but after this initial protest the new invention conducted itself in a most satisfactory manner.

During the autumn a couple of hours or so were devoted daily to ski practice. Nansen, Sverdrup, Johansen, and several others were already expert "skilöbers," and as ski would necessarily play an important part if it should at any time be necessary to retreat on foot over the ice, everybody desired to perfect himself in the art. By this time, too, the puppies were old enough to begin their education, and the business of breaking them to harness was taken in hand in earnest. At first they showed a well-defined aversion to the process; but patience and gentleness prevailed, and in a little while the dogs settled down to their duty as steadily as if they had been at it for years. The canine family had again been increased by eight pups, and with a view to the general comfort, kennels were constructed outside the ship, though the puppies—bright, amusing little fellows—still occupied quarters on board. They had a special turn for investigation, which, being indulged at every opportunity, sometimes led to unfortunate consequences. One luckless pup, while studying the construction of an iron bolt, found occasion to apply his tongue to the metal. The result surprised him: the tongue forthwith froze firmly to the bolt, and pull and back as he would, he could not free himself. Naturally he began to howl piteously, and the noise having brought Nansen and Bentzen to his assistance, the latter, after warming the bolt with his hand, managed to free the victim, who, notwithstanding an exuberant display of gratitude, probably was for a time a sadder if not a wiser dog.

Meanwhile Nansen kept his proposed journey steadily in view. He would have liked Sverdrup for his companion, but both of these two could not properly leave the ship. Then came the question which of them should go. Both were willing, but Nansen being the responsible man of the expedition, decided to take what he considered the more dangerous post himself, and to leave Sverdrup in charge of the *Fram*. Whom, then, should Nansen ask to be his companion? Probably there was not a man on board who would not gladly have accompanied him; but while some could not be spared from their duties, others were not sufficiently at home on ski, and after some consideration he chose Johansen, who in many ways seemed peculiarly well fitted for the work. Before inviting him, however, Nansen, one evening in November when the whole party were together, made known his plan, and pointed out that, whatever credit might fall to the share of those who went on this trip, those who remained with the *Fram* and brought her safely home would be no less worthy of honour.

Preliminaries being thus adjusted, preparations for the great undertaking were actively carried forward. Mogstad and Sverdrup undertook the construction, respectively, of sledges and sleeping-bags, Juell turned his hand to harness-making, the doctor prepared a suitable supply of medicines and simple surgical appliances, and Nansen gave attention to the important subject of clothing.

The twelfth of December was observed as a special festival in honour of the *Fram*; for from observations taken that day, it was found that she had surpassed all competitors, and attained the highest latitude ever reached by any ship—namely, 82° 30′ north. By Christmas Day she had further improved her position, and the knowledge that the eighty-third parallel had been crossed came as a welcome Christmas gift to the crew.

STILL DRIFTING.

The new year was still young when the *Fram* was subjected to the most severe test she had yet had to bear. Early on the morning of the third of January the ice began to creak and groan, and cracks opened in the floe on the port side of the ship in a manner which rendered it desirable at once to secure sundry articles which had hitherto reposed on the ice. While this was being done the immense pressure forced the ice up into a ridge, which, travelling slowly forward in the direction of the pressure, was constantly driven nearer to the ship, and threatened her with unavoidable destruction. Was it possible that she could escape? Things could hardly have looked blacker, and in view of a nip such as that which sent the *Jeannette* to the bottom, sledges, kayaks, provisions for men and dogs, and several tins of oil were brought on deck, whence they could be removed to the ice at a moment's notice.

The pressure and cracking continued throughout the day, and by night the condition of the ice had become so alarming that the men began to fetch up from the hold everything necessary for a retreat over the ice. The dogs, too, needed assistance; for greatly to their alarm, the water having risen over the ice had flooded their house, and they had to be taken on board. No one took off his clothes that night, and as the hours went on "the noise of battle rolled" louder and more deafening as the floes crushed and ground one upon another. So stupendous was the force at work that the ice-ridge on the port side had developed into a huge hummock, which was being driven violently towards the apparently doomed ship.

The approaching monster rose as high as the rail, and as it came nearer and nearer it seemed to every one that the end could not be far off. But De Long's motto was also Nansen's—" Stick to the ship as long as she will stick to us, and when she is ready to leave us, try to be a little readier to leave her;" and in accordance with this maxim, all stores remaining in the hold were brought up, and every one prepared to quit at a moment's notice.

The pressure, however, subsided, and throughout the day the ice remained fairly quiescent. The truce, however, was but a brief one. About eight o'clock in the evening a new assault was made on the unlucky *Fram*, and showers of snow and ice fragments came thundering down upon her. The noise was appalling, and at last Nansen's hopes deserted him. How long would it take the ice to carry out the work of destruction ?

He called everybody on deck and loosed the dogs; but when the prospect looked blackest, suddenly the ice relaxed, and though the *Fram* was half buried beneath the snow and ice which had been forced upon her, the pressure ceased. She was safe, and more than this, close inspection failed to discover that the slightest damage had been received by the stout little ship.

CHAPTER XX.

"A KING OF MIGHTY MEN."

AT the first sign of returning daylight the preparations for the great journey were pushed forward more actively than ever. Sledges and kayaks specially designed for the work were got ready; provisions sufficient to last two men and twenty-eight dogs for several months were carefully selected; guns and scientific instruments were chosen, and everything was done to ensure a successful journey.

By the twenty-sixth of February all was ready: farewells and good wishes were exchanged, and accompanied by Sverdrup and two or three others who meant to start them on their way, the two daring explorers set out. But luck was against them: the sledges showed themselves unequal to the work, and before Sverdrup's party had reached its limit the expedition had to turn back for repairs.

The load was clearly too heavy for convenience, so Nansen, rather than reduce his stores, determined to take six sledges, and two days later he and Johansen, with the same companions as before, again started.

The six sledges proved more unmanageable than the four had done, and though the weight was reduced by the abandonment of several sacks of dog-food, after working hard for several days with no adequate result, the travellers decided to go back. Not that the project was given up—nothing was further from the mind of either Nansen or his comrade—but they believed that when the sun returned travelling would be easier and quicker, as well as pleasanter. An increased rate of speed would allow of a proportionate reduction in the provisions, while at the same time the more the weight was reduced the faster would the dogs be able to travel.

With this end in view Nansen eliminated every unnecessary article from his stores, and reduced the food taken for the dogs to thirty days' supply. This was, he knew, a miserably insufficient amount; but he could not carry more, glad as he would have been to do so. For himself and Johansen he allowed one hundred days' rations, and these, on hygienic grounds, were of a varied nature, and included pemmican, fish-flour, soups, biscuits, butter, oatmeal, whey-powder, chocolate, sugar, and other miscellaneous edibles. Most of these articles were partly cooked, and merely required warming, for which purpose a small cooker and a supply of petroleum for its use were added to the outfit.

Clothing was confined within the narrowest possible limits. Furs being voted too warm for ordinary use, were eschewed altogether, and the explorers contented themselves with thick woollen underclothing, knickerbockers and gaiters of stout Norwegian homespun, camel's-hair coats, thick jerseys, and wolfskin gloves. In addition to these, each man had an outside suit of wind and snow proof canvas, a soft felt hat, and for foot-wear warm socks and "finnesko" or "komager," with stout soles of well-tarred sealskin.

The tent, of the thinnest possible silk, seemed hardly suitable for Arctic work, for it had no floor, and only weighed about three pounds; but with a warm fur sleeping-bag, this slight shelter sufficed for the needs of these "hardy Norsemen."

The rest of the equipment consisted of scientific instruments, firearms and ammunition, a small medicine-chest, several pairs of ski, a spare shirt apiece, and sundry miscellaneous articles, including a Kodak photographic apparatus—the whole being packed on three sledges.

On the fourteenth of March the explorers once more set out, and this time there was no need to return. A few miles from the ship they said good-bye to those of their comrades who had come thus far with them, and then, resolutely turning their backs on comfort, civilization, and human society, they went forward alone to face the perils and hardships of the unknown, mysterious realm of ice.

For a few days everything prospered; even the ice seemed well disposed to the undertaking, and the level snow-covered floes extending for miles afforded excellent travelling. If it would but continue, there could be little difficulty in reaching the Pole; but this easy life was too good to last.

The first trouble was the collapse of one of the dogs. He became too ill and weak to work, and after a couple of days, as he showed no signs of recovery, he was killed to provide a supper for the rest of the team. This was a hard task for the tender-hearted Norwegians, but it could not be helped; though most of the dogs refused to touch the meat, and it was only later on, when compelled by hunger to eat anything, that some of them conquered their aversion to this cannibal fare.

Day after day the difficulties and hardships of the journey increased. Level floes gave place to rough, hummocky ice, where the sledges were perpetually sticking fast or capsizing; and sometimes water lanes opened unexpectedly, and the explorers had to go far out of their way to get round or over the openings. But hindrances notwithstanding, progress was made, and every time they took an observation for latitude they found that they had improved their position. As the sun rose higher they took to travelling indifferently by day or night, starting when convenient, and leaving off when they or the dogs were too exhausted to go further.

Nansen, who officiated as cook, was always astir first in order to prepare breakfast. This process

"A KING OF MIGHTY MEN." 195

usually took about an hour, and he then aroused Johansen; and sitting up in the sleeping-bag, the two partook of chocolate, bread and butter, and pemmican, or, as a variety, oatmeal porridge, or a compound of flour, water, and butter, with whey-powder dissolved in hot water as a substitute for tea. When the meal was finished, any needful work, such as the repairing of clothes, harness, or provision-bags, received attention, and then the dogs were harnessed and the march began.

When the ice was too rough for straightforward travelling, Nansen went on in advance to find a route through the chaos of hummocks and ridges. Close behind him came his dogs with their sledge, while Johansen, with the two other teams and sledges, followed in their wake. Very often the roughness of the ice was altogether too much for the dogs, and over and over again in the course of every march the men were forced to haul or lift the sledges over obstructions which their canine assistants could not surmount unaided. As time went on and the dogs grew weaker, this happened oftener and oftener, until the explorers spent a large portion of their time in going backwards and forwards leading the way—helping here, hauling there, lifting, shouting, encouraging, rating, and when all else failed, belabouring the exhausted dogs. To thrash them seemed cruel, merciless, but there was no help for it; they must go on, or the expedition must fail abjectly. Anything was better than that, so day after day dragged its length along in one eternal round of hauling, shouting, thrashing, contriving, and toiling to the utmost limit of strength and endurance. Day after day, too, the patient dogs bravely struggled forward with their loads.

After starting in the morning the travellers plodded on steadily for several hours, and then came a short halt for lunch; but very often the cold robbed the meal of most of its comfort, and the only chance of outwitting the cutting wind, which had a genius for penetrating everything, was to take refuge in the sleeping-bag. Time would not allow of a long stop, and once more getting under way, the plucky fellows and their much-enduring dogs went on, though towards the end of a march they grew so weary that as often as not they fell asleep while walking. To make matters worse, the intense cold—about seventy degrees of frost—froze the woollen clothes into a species of armour which only relaxed when the warmth of the sleeping-bag temporarily reduced the garments to a damp condition resembling that so picturesquely described by Mr. Mantalini. Once outside the bag the clothes speedily became as stiff as ever, and in course of time Nansen's sleeves cut deep into his wrists, causing sores which did not heal for months.

When the day's march ended the dogs' labours were over for the time, and while Johansen fed and tended them, Nansen pitched the tent, built a snow wall

"A KING OF MIGHTY MEN." 197

round it to keep out the wind, and cooked the supper. This consisted sometimes of stewed pemmican and potatoes, sometimes of a compound of fish-flour, butter, and meal, known as *fiskegratin*, sometimes of soup, biscuit, and pemmican, washed down by a jorum of hot water flavoured with whey-powder.

Cooking was rather a long business, and while it was in progress the worn-out men, with shivering frames and chattering teeth, vainly attempted to get a little warmth into their half-frozen bodies. Hot food and drink did something towards warming them, though not unfrequently they were too tired to keep awake long enough to eat their well-earned supper, and fell asleep with the food half-way to their mouths. But the time for slumber was all too short, and after a few hours of rest the round of work began again, with its one item of satisfaction—that their toil and suffering were not all in vain, for each day they camped a little nearer to the Pole.

By the fourth of April they had reached 86° 2′ north latitude. This, though far beyond any point achieved by previous expeditions, was nevertheless a disappointing result of so much labour, for the distance traversed daily ought to have resulted in the attainment of a much higher latitude. It was clear to Nansen that while they were advancing northward the ice was drifting southward, though at a somewhat slower rate, and this being the case, it would be quite impossible to reach the Pole in the time at their disposal. If they had had the dogs from the Olenek with them, the work could no doubt have been accomplished; but they were far away in Siberia, and time spent in wishing for them was merely so much time wasted.

After four days more of toil, the travellers found that they had made but little progress: 86° 13·6′ north was their exact latitude. At this point the ice was all but impassable, and from the highest hummock in the neighbourhood Nansen could see, stretching away until sight failed in the distance, a limitless expanse of rough ice, scored by cracks and water lanes, and intersected by ridges and hummocks, varied here and there by snow-drifts in which sledges must infallibly capsize, and dogs and men half bury themselves. "Confusion worse confounded" reigned supreme, and as he gazed across the chaotic Polar ice-field, he came to the conclusion that, with the resources at their command, he and Johansen were attempting an impossible task, and spending time, strength, energy, and suffering in an endeavour which must be futile. It was a useless waste, and unwilling as he was to leave anything unfinished to which he set his hand, he then and there decided to turn his back on the Pole and shape a course for Franz Josef Land, where any spare time could be profitably employed in exploration. It was, of course, disappointing to fall short of complete success, but after all much had been done. Of all the mighty men who

"A KING OF MIGHTY MEN." 199

had entered on the great field of Polar discovery Nansen had proved himself the king: the world's record was broken, and for all practical purposes the Arctic problem was solved.

On the eighth of April the southward march began, and after a day or two the travelling greatly improved. The route now lay south-westward, apparently in the same general direction as that taken by the ridges and water lanes; so that, instead of perpetually crossing them, the track ran parallel with them. This saved a great deal of trouble, and long marches were made. One of unusual length led to rather unfortunate results; for when it ended, so many hours had elapsed since the travellers last camped that both their watches had run down. This was a grave misfortune, for they carried no other chronometer; and though Nansen put the timepieces right as well as he could, the result of observations for longitude thenceforward contained an element of vagueness that was very far from satisfactory.

The dogs' food was now rapidly diminishing, and though most of the team had manifested a great aversion to eating their companions, Nansen decided to begin killing off the weakest dogs, and thus save a small stock of pemmican for possible future needs. To the explorers themselves killing the faithful, hardworking dogs was a most hateful task, and the necessity of butchering them with a knife made it more horrible than it would have been had the stock of ammunition been large enough to warrant the expenditure of any cartridges for the purpose.

About the end of April the ice deteriorated considerably, and travelling became almost as bad as ever. Sometimes snow-storms kept the party in camp, but most troublesome of all were the numerous water lanes and pools, sometimes open, and sometimes coated with ice too weak to bear and too thick for the kayaks to penetrate, even had they been in a usable condition. The frequent upsets, however, which they had suffered had caused leaks innumerable; and as many hours' work would be required to put the kayaks in order, Nansen saw no use in wasting time on them until it was absolutely necessary to do so. This was not the case at present, though going round the pools took up time, and added considerably to the labours of the march.

The gradual diminution of the dog-team did not mend matters. By the middle of May only twelve dogs remained, and as these were not enough to draw three sledges, the now greatly-reduced loads were rearranged so as to admit of one sledge being broken up for firewood. With only two sledges to look after, progress was easier; but as a set-off to this, the increasing weakness of the dogs made them daily less able to cope with the difficulties of the way, and they were in constant need of help. The two men had to work as hard, or harder, than ever; for only on level ice could the dogs get on alone, though, willing as

THE FIRST WHALE. Page 201.

ever, they still did their best, and sometimes worked until, utterly worn out, they could do no more, and fell inert and helpless in their tracks. For such faithful service death was a poor reward, although, like the canine heroes they were, they died in doing their duty.

On the sixteenth of May an unusually large pool covered with thin ice gave a good deal of trouble, and hardly had it been passed when the disgusted travellers reached another of equal dimensions, covered, like its predecessor, with the thinnest of ice. This was too much of a good thing, and the explorers decided to camp, hoping that a night's frost would make the ice strong enough to bear. Before they settled down, an unaccustomed noise attracted Nansen's attention. He went to discover the cause, and as he gazed up came a whale, followed by another and another, until the pool was dotted with black, ungainly heads. A whale would be a godsend. Off he ran for his gun and a harpoon; but before he got back the whales had departed. He heard them blowing in the distance, and followed the sound, but could not get near enough to effect a capture. A day's delay might very likely have enabled him to secure one, but time was too valuable. It was consoling, though, to be once more in a region where animal life existed. Further north no living thing had come to break the death-like solitude. Not long afterwards more whales, a seal, and some birds made their appearance, and, better still, the fresh tracks of several bears were seen in the snow.

A day or two later the water lanes and pools became so wide and occurred so often that the repair of the kayaks could no longer be delayed. The work took some days; but already that peculiar appearance of the sky which in the Polar regions always indicates either land or open water had been noticed, and letting alone the convenience of having boats in which to ferry across the lanes, it was probable that they would soon be wanted for more extended voyaging.

On the eighth of June the repairs were completed, camp was broken up, and the journey continued over villainous ice. The lanes, under the influence of a strong wind, had to a great extent closed up, but those which still existed were crammed with broken ice-fragments, sometimes, though not always, packed close enough to bear. Even the solid ice was covered deeply with a sludgy mixture of half-frozen snow and water, through which the dogs floundered somehow, half swimming and half walking. It was not surprising that some of them became paralyzed; and by the middle of the month only three were left alive.

Food was now becoming scarce, and had to be used sparingly. The dogs and their masters were alike hungry, when one day Johansen had the luck to shoot a seal, which Nansen harpooned in time to prevent it from sinking. It was soon hauled on to the ice, and

"A KING OF MIGHTY MEN."

in a wonderfully short time a good meal of seal-meat was being cooked. For the first time in many days, there was really enough for men and dogs to eat, and thus refreshed and strengthened they went on their way rejoicing.

The next seal-hunt was less generally successful. The kayaks had just been launched on a big pool, with the sledges and dogs on board, when a loud splash was heard. Guessing the cause, Nansen sprang ashore, and a moment afterwards Johansen from his kayak shot the seal through the head. Nansen, who was hauling up one of the sledges, seized a harpoon, and as the seal floated quietly for a few seconds, drove it deep into the creature's back. While he was thus engaged, the sledge, which he had left to take care of itself, slipped down the ice, sent the kayaks, Johansen, and the dogs adrift, and completed its round of mischief by partially capsizing the whole concern, and sliding far enough into the water to drench its own load. The kayaks, which fortunately were still close to the edge of the ice, promptly began to fill, and the cooker and sundry ski floated off on their own account. Nansen meanwhile was holding on with all his might to the seal, but strong as he was, that animal was more than he could manage single-handed; and as Johansen could neither right his rapidly-filling kayak nor get out of it unaided, Nansen had to leave the seal and go to his assistance. The kayak was dragged up safely, and then the two men hauled the seal on to the ice. There was now time to recover the errant cooker and ski, and to investigate the condition of the maltreated stores. Wonderfully little damage had been done, considering that everything had been under water; even the paper-cased cartridges were merely wet outside, and the biscuit and some loose powder seemed to be the only things materially the worse for their ducking. Altogether the explorers had cause to congratulate themselves, especially as they were rapidly acquiring a genuine Arctic relish for seal in every form. The meat was voted good, the blubber excellent, and blood-pancakes a most agreeable change.

A few days after this adventure, the snow, which had been steadily deteriorating, attained to such perfection of badness that further progress was impossible, and the travellers camped to wait until either frost or rain should improve the condition of the ice. There was now no need to hurry, for another seal having been shot, food was abundant; so they rested contentedly in camp, occupying themselves with calking the leaky kayaks, and painting them with a pleasing compound of soot and train-oil. Burnt bone dust, after making a hideous stink while in preparation, proved a ghastly failure when used as a pigment.

One evening Kaifas, Nansen's dog, began to bark so furiously outside the tent that his master looked out to see what was the matter. A bear! In less than no time Nansen's gun was levelled, and the ball struck the bear in the shoulder, laming but not disabling her, and off she went, followed by two cubs, which had been waiting for her at a little distance. Thanks to her broken shoulder, Nansen was just able to keep pace with her, and at length getting a good opportunity he fired again, this time with fatal effect, for the bear fell. The cubs, utterly nonplussed at their mother's unwonted conduct, ran round and round, vainly trying to induce her to rise, and growing more and more puzzled and unhappy, until another shot stretched one of them helpless and growling beside its dying mother. The remaining cub, knowing something was wrong, but quite unable to understand what it might be, stood looking sadly from one to the other, and evidently indifferent to what fate might have in store for it. As Nansen came up it made no attempt either to escape or to defend itself, and another bullet through the heart speedily ended its life and its sorrows.

Several times while in camp Nansen saw something in the distance which looked like snow-fields. Could it be land? It hardly seemed possible, for surely no land could be so completely snow-covered as not to leave a single rock visible; and believing that what he saw was merely a cloud-bank, he troubled himself no more about it. In the course of a few days the kayaks were satisfactorily finished, and the stores having been overhauled, everything that could possibly be spared was turned out, and another start was made. Two days later—the twenty-fourth of July—the cloud-like snow-field assumed a definite form; there could no longer be any doubt that a snow-clad land lay at no great distance, though what it could be neither of the explorers knew.

Appearances were deceptive. The newly-found land seemed to be quite near, and the telescope showed rocky peaks rising above the snow; but day after day passed, and still the travellers journeyed wearily over the ice, without, as it seemed, materially reducing their distance from the wished-for shore. To add to Nansen's discomforts, a sharp attack of lumbago now almost disabled him. For some days walking was a distinctly penitential exercise, and at camping-time he had to invoke the aid of his companion to change his shoes and socks.

During this part of the journey Johansen met with an adventure which narrowly escaped having a serious ending. While launching the kayaks to cross a water lane, Nansen heard a noise, and turning round saw his comrade on his back in the snow. Above him stood a huge bear, a cuff from whose paw had knocked him down; but being a powerful fellow, he had caught the bear by the throat, and held him at arm's length. Nansen sprang to get his gun, which was in its case in the kayak; but as he did so the little craft slid down into the water, and heavily laden as it was, it was as much as he could do to haul it up. Meanwhile Johansen gripped the bear's throat with all his strength, but Bruin was too strong for him; and

"A KING OF MIGHTY MEN." 207

while Nansen was still busy getting his gun out of the kayak, he heard a quiet voice exhorting him to hurry up unless he wanted to be too late. At that moment the bear caught sight of Kaifas, and leaving Johansen turned to attack the dog, to whom he administered one or two hearty cuffs before Nansen succeeded in disengaging his gun and ending the conflict with a well-directed shot. Wonderful to say, Johansen came off almost scot-free, the only traces he bore of the ignominious treatment he had received being a scratch on one hand and a white patch on his cheek where the bear's paw had wiped off the accumulated grime.

All things in this world—even ice-fields—have an end, and at last the two explorers stood on the edge of the pack, its white, monotonous expanse stretching away behind them, the blue waters of old ocean lapping at their feet, while before them lay the land on which their hopes and thoughts had so long been centred. But even in their joy a note of sadness mingled, for heavily laden as the kayaks must be, to take the two remaining dogs further was impossible. Those two, who had followed them so far and so faithfully, held a very warm place in their masters' affections, and it was with sad hearts that, having loaded up the kayaks with the sledges and other gear, they said farewell to their canine friends, and each shot his comrade's dog.

CHAPTER XXI.

FRANZ JOSEF LAND AND HOME.

A FAVOURABLE wind was now blowing which quickly wafted the travellers across the strip of open water intervening between the edge of the ice and the land, and they were soon paddling along the face of a mighty glacier which rose like a wall of ice sheer up from the sea. No such thing as a practicable landing-place was to be seen, so when camping-time came the explorers took refuge on a convenient floe. This sort of work continued for several days; for the land was merely a chain of ice-clad islands, between which the sea was covered with level ice, varied here and there by sheets of open water, so that the explorers' time was pretty equally divided between boating and hauling. One day the kayaks were in some danger from a couple of aggressive walruses; but a ball from Johansen's gun drove away one, wounded and bellowing, and a still more successful shot of Nansen's killed the second. It was no easy matter to get a knife into the thick hide, but the feat was accomplished at last, and some strips of

FRANZ JOSEF LAND AND HOME.

meat and blubber were added to the stock of provisions.

That same evening, for the first time, land was reached—real land—sand, stones, earth; and, to the intense delight of the travellers, they found in a sheltered corner a bed of beautiful green moss bejewelled with bright-tinted Arctic flowers. On this spot—the first land which for two long years the wanderers' feet had pressed—the Norwegian flag was hoisted, and beneath their national banner they held a banquet of the best that they had, in honour of this far northern land, now for the first time seen by mortal eyes.

Though this newly-discovered island group lacked the softer graces of more southern lands, nature had in some respects dealt kindly with it. At one island blue wavelets, so clear that every stone and sea-urchin at the bottom could be plainly seen, lapped gently on the level shell-strewn beach; while at the foot of the cliffs patches of beautiful rose-coloured snow relieved the all-prevailing whiteness, and the cliffs themselves served as an orchestra for a chorus of unmusically-voiced little auks, and a bevy of snow-buntings fluttered and hopped fearlessly from stone to stone. Nor were these the only birds proper to the locality, for scores of the rarely-seen Ross's gull were flying about, evidently perfectly at home. To Nansen—a most ardent zoologist—this discovery was specially interesting, as the breeding-place of these little-known birds was now discovered for the first time.

Of more practical utility was the discovery of bear-tracks crossing the snow in every direction. Not that the tracks could in themselves serve any useful purpose, but bear-tracks implied bears, and Nansen was lucky enough to shoot a remarkably fine specimen of the race just as the stock of meat reached an unpleasantly low ebb.

Storms and contrary winds kept the travellers stationary for about a week, and then, suddenly changing its tactics, the wind drifted the floe on which they were encamped far out to sea. Fortunately the water was now fairly open, and they once more took to the kayaks, until, a couple of days later, ice and wind again combined against them. This time land—barren and uninviting, but still land, and a safe refuge—was available, and the kayaks were hauled up the beach, in the hope that a long stay would be as unnecessary as it was undesirable. But by the next morning the ice was packed close against the beach, and seemed to have come to stay; so a temporary shelter was constructed of loose stones roofed in with the tent spread on ski and bamboo poles. The result was a structure afterwards known as the den, in which Nansen's long legs were unable to find accommodation, and he had to sleep with his feet outside the door.

The delay proved fatal to any further advance

that season. The summer was drawing to a close, and new ice would soon begin to form; so, as game seemed fairly plentiful, the travellers decided to winter where they were, and at once set about building a more commodious domicile. The first thing, however, was to lay in a stock of food, and for a few days they contented themselves with the den as a sleeping-place, and occupied their time in hunting. While so employed they met with sundry adventures. One day, while skinning a walrus on the ice at some distance from land, Nansen happened to look towards the shore, and saw to his dismay that the floe on which they were standing had become detached from the shore ice, and was rapidly drifting seawards. By a lucky chance they had the kayaks and sledges with them, so hurriedly cutting off a supply of meat and blubber, they flung their spoil into the kayaks, and paddled hard for the shore against a strong wind. It was all they could do to make headway, and the frail boats were in constant peril of being crushed by the enormous blocks of ice, which were swirling around and dashing up against one another in a style most unpleasantly suggestive of what might be expected should they happen to collide with one of the boats. But no accident happened, and at last the kayaks were safely beached. Fate, however, seemed to have a spite against that walrus-meat, for the place where it was stored was afterwards raided by bears. The robbers, however, paid the penalty with their lives; so, on the whole, the explorers gained by the transaction. Other hunting excursions were more successful, and in the course of a week or two a large stock of meat, both bear and walrus, had been accumulated. It was an unusually good time for the gulls; for while the men were busy skinning and cutting up the game, the hungry birds came fearlessly crowding round them, snatching scraps from under their feet and quarrelling noisily over choice morsels.

Gulls and bears, however, were not the only robbers; the foxes of that locality were confirmed kleptomaniacs, and carried off everything, not caring in the least whether they could make the slightest use of it or not. Pieces of bamboo, wire and stones, harpoons and twine, all disappeared, and finally those indiscriminating thieves made off with the thermometer, an instrument which could not be of the smallest possible use to them.

A stock of meat having been secured, the next thing was to build a hut for the winter. All that could be attempted was to construct a shelter big enough for two men, and sufficiently weather-proof to keep out the winter cold. Of pretensions to architectural beauty it had none: there was but one room, which served alike for kitchen, sitting-room, and bedchamber, and the walls, constructed of stones banked round with earth and snow, were only about three feet high. The deficiency in height was counteracted by hollowing out the floor so as to allow even Nansen to stand upright. The hut was then roofed in with walrus hides and driftwood, the whole being thickly covered with snow. A chimney of iceblocks completed the edifice; and when the crevices had been carefully calked with moss, it was really not uncomfortable, though it might have been better had the stones, which were the only available substitute for bed, couch, and chairs, been a trifle smoother and softer.

As soon as the hut was completed, Nansen and his companion again turned their attention to hunting; and before the sun disappeared on the fifteenth of October, they had laid in a supply of meat sufficient to serve for the winter. Bears were all very well, but skinning walrus was a most unpleasant business; for the creatures were so heavy that it was next to impossible to drag them out of the water, and in attempting to obtain the hide and blubber without landing the original owner, the two men fairly saturated their clothes with oil and dirt. To clean them was next to impossible, but by boiling and scraping them a considerable amount of fat was extracted which afterwards served for the lamp. As the light disappeared and work became impossible, eating and sleeping were the only practicable employments, and often for days together neither of the men put his head outside the door, unless to fetch in a supply of ice or meat for themselves or some blubber for the lamp, which was always kept burning.

Nansen had hoped to get through a good deal of work during the winter, but the difficulties were enormous; for whenever he touched a piece of paper with hands or clothes, the result was the appearance of a brown patch whereon it was useless to attempt to write. Cleanliness was an impossible virtue: the only substitute for soap was moss and sand, or occasionally bear's blood and train-oil; but none of these was universally applicable, and hands, faces, hair, and clothes gradually deepened in colour to a rich black, very far removed from the fair hair and complexion with which nature had endowed the Norwegians. At Christmas Johansen attempted to celebrate the festival by a general clean-up. Having turned all rubbish out of the hut, he proceeded further to put his outside shirt inside; and Nansen having followed his example, further improved the occasion by an attempt to wash in a small drop of hot water. This incessant and inevitable dirt was one of the explorers' worst troubles and discomforts; for not only were the oil-soaked garments very ineffectual in keeping out the cold, but wherever they touched the skin they stuck and caused sores.

Winter wore away by degrees, and in spite of discomforts both Nansen and Johansen enjoyed excellent health, except for a few days about the beginning of February, when Nansen had a sharp attack of rheumatism. Fortunately they managed to sleep away a good deal of their time; otherwise the hours might have passed rather slowly, seeing that the only things they possessed in the shape of literature were a navigation table and an almanac. It was lucky, too, that neither of the travellers ever tired of bear, varied occasionally by a little burnt blubber abstracted from the lamp, though some flour and sugar would have been agreeable additions to the bill of fare.

The sun reappeared at the end of February, and a few days later a couple of bears were shot. Nansen now began to think of moving on, but before a start could be made there was much to be done. First of all new clothes were required, and these were constructed of blankets sewn with thread obtained by unravelling canvas. A bearskin sleeping-bag was also made, and a few provisions which still remained out of the supply brought from the *Fram* were dug out of the cache where they had been stored during the winter. These, unfortunately, had been spoiled by the damp, and very little was still fit for use; so a stock of bear-meat was substituted for the damaged edibles, and the petroleum-tins were filled with train-oil. The sledges and kayaks were overhauled, and any necessary repairs were made. But the tent was altogether past mending, and the intending travellers had to make up their minds to sleep as best they could in the open air, or sheltered by the sledges and kayaks banked round with snow and covered in with the sail. Finally the hut was photographed both outside and inside, and then at seven p.m. on the nineteenth of May the homeward journey began.

The next month was spent in alternate boating across open water and hauling the sledges over flat ice. Occasionally a storm caused some delay, and once or twice provisions ran short; but when this happened, a walrus or a bear generally appeared, and was secured at the most opportune moment. Not that adventures were scarce; indeed, this was, perhaps, one of the most adventurous parts of the whole journey. Once, after sailing all day along the shore of one of the islands, the two kayaks were moored, safely, as their owners thought, to a large block of ice, and thus secured were left to take care of themselves while the two men went ashore. After a while they looked back. The boats were gone! and looking seawards, Nansen saw to his dismay that they had broken from their mooring, and were rapidly drifting from the shore. What was to be done? Everything—provisions, sleeping-bag, guns, ammunition, sledges—was on board. Those kayaks *must* be recovered. It was the work of a very few moments to rush to the shore, and throwing off some of his outer clothing, Nansen dashed into the ice-cold water. He was a good swimmer; but the kayaks were already some distance off, and it was all he could do to reach them. Long before he did so the cold began to take hold of him, his limbs became stiffer and stiffer, every stroke was more difficult, but as he looked ahead he saw that the distance was decreasing. Yes; a little more patience, and he and Johansen would be safe. At last the long swim was accomplished, and stretching out his arm, Nansen caught hold of one of the ski, which was firmly lashed across the stern. But his stiffened limbs refused to act, and it was with the greatest difficulty that he contrived to drag himself on board.

His troubles were not yet over. In order to carry the sledges more conveniently, the two kayaks were lashed side by side, and it was no easy matter to paddle; but half frozen as he was, Nansen managed to overcome this difficulty also, and shivering and shaking with cold he at last reached the edge of the ice. Johansen, who meanwhile had been restlessly pacing up and down, equally powerless to help and to stand still, was at hand to help him, and having hauled the kayaks into a place of safety, he assisted Nansen to strip off his wet clothing and to put on such dry things as he had. Once in the sleeping-bag he soon got warm, and after two or three hours' sleep was quite ready to do his share towards demolishing the supper which Johansen had prepared.

A couple of days later, while peacefully sailing along, Nansen's kayak was attacked by a walrus. More than once the monsters had fallen foul of the frail craft, which they apparently regarded as some new and unknown kind of beast calling for instant destruction, but so far their hostile endeavours had been unattended by success. This walrus, however, had no intention of failing. Up he came with a bang against the kayak, and then, while endeavouring to drag it under water with his flipper, thrust his long tusks inside, just missing Nansen's leg. A blow on the head from the paddle greatly astonished the aggressor. At first he contemplated smashing Nansen, but more mature consideration led to the abandonment of this scheme, and he somewhat hastily retired into the depths. The kayak by this time was nearly full of water, for the walrus's tusk had cut a long rent in its canvas covering, and its occupant had barely time to scramble to a neighbouring floe and drag his damaged boat after him. This mishap entailed several hours' work in repairing the kayak and in drying its thoroughly-soaked cargo, none of which, fortunately, was much the worse for its ducking.

Having dried their property, the travellers made ready for another start, when Nansen, who in the intervals of cooking a late breakfast had ascended a hummock to look around him, thought he heard a dog barking. At first he did not feel quite sure; so many loons and other birds were calling to one another with unmelodious voices, that it was no easy matter to distinguish the sounds. Then came the bark again: surely no mortal bird, however croaky its note, could emit such a sound; that bark could only have emanated from a canine throat.

Down rushed Nansen and awakened Johansen, who was still peacefully sleeping. "I have heard dogs," he shouted. But Johansen at first quite declined to believe that his companion had done anything of the sort, and as Nansen was not to be shaken in his faith that dogs and presumably human beings were in the neighbourhood, it was finally agreed that he should go to reconnoitre while Johansen stayed at the camp to look after their joint belongings. Accordingly, as soon as breakfast had been hastily gulped down, Nansen, gun in hand, set out on his ski. He had not gone far before he again heard that welcome bark, and following the sound, he soon espied a man walking among some distant hummocks.

The intervening distance was soon covered, and as Nansen drew nearer he thought that in the figure before him he recognized Mr. Frederick G. Jackson, whom he had met in London, and who now was in charge of an English expedition which had for nearly two years been engaged in the exploration of Franz Josef Land. After all, the world is a little place. Who would have expected to meet a casual acquaintance in the wilds of Franz Josef Land? Evidently Jackson had not, though he heartily shook the grimy explorer by the hand, saying as he did so, "I'm awfully glad to see you."

"So am I to see you," responded Nansen cordially; and then, in answer to the other's question, proceeded to explain that his ship was not there, and that he had one companion who was keeping camp some distance off. Meanwhile Jackson had been steadily looking at his interlocutor; something in the voice and figure seemed familiar, though the fair-haired Scandinavian whom Jackson had seen in London bore little resemblance to the shaggy, dirty, unkempt object now under contemplation.

"Aren't you Nansen?" he exclaimed.

"Yes, I am Nansen," replied the new-comer tranquilly.

"By Jove, I really am awfully glad to see you," answered Jackson; and then the two fell to shaking hands again with renewed heartiness.

The two explorers, still eagerly conversing, then set out for Elmwood, Jackson's headquarters; but before they reached the house, the Englishmen, who had quickly guessed the identity of Jackson's companion, turned out in force to meet them and give him a hearty welcome. Then having given three thundering cheers for Nansen and his achievement, two or three of the party went off in search of Johansen, while the others convoyed Nansen to the house, where in due time Johansen also arrived.

Then came that long-desired pleasure of a good wash, clean clothes, a shave, and a hair-cut, after which the heroes of the evening, now somewhat more civilized in appearance than they had been an hour or two earlier, sat down to a really sumptuous repast. Midnight was long past; but such occasions as this do

NANSEN ON HIS ARRIVAL AT ELMWOOD.
(From a Photograph by Frederick Jackson.)

not occur every day, and nobody was disposed to take any account of the flight of time.

After a few days' rest Nansen was ready to continue his journey to Spitzbergen. Johansen, however, was too well pleased with his quarters to have any desire to leave them so soon, and as Jackson was very anxious that the two Norwegians should stay at Elmwood until the arrival of his ship, the *Windward*, after due consideration Nansen consented to remain. Several weeks passed pleasantly in hunting, shooting, map-making, fossil-seeking, and such like occupations, and Johansen took advantage of the opportunity to perfect himself in English, of which language he knew very little. The new-comers soon settled down with their hosts, and took their part quite naturally in the daily work and amusements of the English explorers; but thoughts of home were uppermost in their minds, and it was a welcome surprise when, early on the morning of the twenty-sixth of July, the *Windward* dropped anchor in front of the settlement.

Nansen's adventures were now practically at an end. In less than a week the *Windward* discharged the stores which she had brought, and letters and telegrams having been written by those not yet homeward bound, on the seventh of August Nansen and Johansen, with a few of Mr. Jackson's men who were going to England, went on board. Luck still attended them. There was plenty of ice about—quite enough to give trouble; but Captain Brown, who commanded the *Windward*, handled his ship in a masterly manner, and she reached Vardö on the thirteenth of August, six days after she left Franz Josef Land. A telegram quickly flashed the news of Nansen's return through the length and breadth of the land, and after a short stay at that northern port the explorers took their departure for Hammerfest, where Nansen expected to meet his wife.

CHAPTER XXII.

ON BOARD THE "FRAM."

WHEN Nansen and Johansen started on their adventurous journey, they left the *Fram* fast held in the embrace of the ice. It was not very long since that embrace had been a great deal too close to be pleasant; but the grip had relaxed, and for about a month after Nansen left the ship the ice remained quiet, and life went on in the same old monotonous way as it had done before the bustle of the start stirred the voyagers into unwonted activity. At that time the ship was drifting very slowly; but towards the end of April things became more lively, and the ice moved north-westwards at a fair rate. Then came contrary winds, which during the summer drifted the ship backward; but as autumn came on and the wind changed, the *Fram* was once more carried north-westward. She reached her highest point—85° 57′ north latitude—on the sixteenth of October 1895, and from that time forward slowly but surely drifted south-westward.

Before Nansen left the ship he had given Sverdrup

a paper of instructions for his guidance in almost every conceivable emergency, and in accordance with this, Sverdrup, always loyal to his leader, occupied himself and his companions during the greater part of the summer in making preparations for leaving the *Fram* should it be necessary to take to the ice. With this end in view, kayaks, sledges, and ski were prepared, and everything which forethought could suggest was done to ensure the safety, not only of the members of the party themselves, but also that of the records, photographs, and scientific memoranda.

A good deal of time was also spent in liberating the *Fram* from the ice, and the huge hummock which had been formed by the ice-pressure of January was removed. Just as this was accomplished the ice around the ship broke up, and though she was still held fast, open water came within a few feet of her. As time went on this water lane became wider and wider, and the ice by degrees broke away from the *Fram*, leaving her so near the water that when a judiciously-placed mine was exploded near her stern it set her free, and for the first time in nearly two years she was afloat in blue water. She still held the position of a prisoner on parole, for the sphere in which she was at liberty to move was extremely circumscribed; but with some trouble she was warped into a safe dock, where in the course of a few days she was again frozen in.

Everything by this time was ready for a start if

it should seem desirable to leave the *Fram;* but there was little fear that this would become necessary. In fact, when she was again frozen in, there seemed to be every probability that her crew must spend another winter on board, and all preparations were made for so doing. In one respect, however, this winter would be less comfortable than the two preceding ones; for owing partly to one of the cog-wheels of the windmill having worn out, and partly to the necessity of converting portions of the machinery into ski and sledge-runners, the electric apparatus was no longer in working order, and for the remainder of the voyage the ship's company would have to content themselves with oil-lamps.

During the winter, in spite of the absence of the electric light, the time passed comfortably enough. Still the same round of work and duties continued, and all observations were taken as regularly as when Nansen was on board. Certainly life did grow rather monotonous, and the sight of the same faces day after day at length became so trying that the men sought relief in long solitary walks over the ice. It was fortunate that some dogs still remained; there were, in fact, more now than when Nansen left the ship, for several of the pups had pups of their own, whose freaks and frolics were a fruitful source of interest and amusement. Owing to one cause and another several of these pups were seized with convulsions, and in spite of all efforts to relieve them several died.

On the twenty-eighth of February two bears approached the ship, and as some fresh meat was then most desirable, a savoury dish of fried onions was displayed to entice them within convenient range. The bait took, and as they came shambling alongside, a couple of well-aimed shots rolled them over on the ice. Polar bears, however, are not to be disposed of so easily, and they were soon up again trying to make off; but another bullet apiece from Sverdrup's rifle, though not fatal in either case, helped to retard progress, and both bears were eventually secured by their pursuers. These were the first that had been shot for about sixteen months, but during the summer sixteen or seventeen more were killed.

On the fourth of March the sun reappeared above the horizon, and as the days lengthened preparations were made for the joyful day when the *Fram* would get clear of the ice. During the winter she had been slowly but steadily drifting southwards, and by the middle of February had reached 84° 20′ north latitude and 24° east longitude. This was a gain of more than a degree of southing on her October position; but here, owing to adverse winds, she stuck fast until May. Then she again drifted southward, and a week or two later experienced heavy ice-pressure, which increased and decreased as the tide rose and fell. This time, though the ship was lifted from six to nine feet whenever the ice closed upon her, the movement was so silent that when it occurred at night it did not awaken even the lightest sleepers. Meanwhile the coal and other stores which for many months had reposed on the floe were again taken on board, and the engine was cleaned and put in order. All that now remained to be done was to get free. But how was this to be accomplished?

The obvious course was to blow up the ice, and as soon as it began to slacken, a mine of nearly a hundredweight of gunpowder was exploded with such satisfactory results that it really seemed as if another explosion would free the ship. A heavy charge was therefore inserted in the log-line hole; but though the blast resulted in a perfect cataract of ice and water, the *Fram* still remained hard and fast in the pack.

Sundry other mines were exploded with no perceptible effect, though one of them nearly caused a very serious accident to Sverdrup and another man. They had laid their charge, and had just set light to the fuse, when the ice on which they stood suddenly collapsed, and let them down into the water most unpleasantly near the mine. They struggled hard to scramble out; but the steep, slippery ice was not easy to climb, and it was only after the greatest exertion that they managed to get out of danger just before the charge exploded. After a few more blasts the ship was so far freed that she was set afloat; but the pool in which she lay was enclosed by miles of ice, and for all practical purposes she might almost as well have been still hard held.

The pool, however, was the forerunner of many more openings, and by dint of hard work and watchfulness little by little the *Fram* was forced through the ice. Progress, of course, was very slow—two or three miles a day was considered quite an achievement; very often the way was blocked altogether, and the ship held captive for hours, and sometimes for days. This sort of work continued until the thirteenth of August, when at midnight the ice slackened so much that Sverdrup succeeded in forcing the *Fram* through the pack and into open water.

There was now nothing to do but to steer for home, and on the twentieth of August the *Fram* cast anchor at Skjærvö in Finmark. A few days before she had spoken the *Söstrene*, a schooner from Tromsö, but her captain not having heard of Nansen's return had no good news to give. Sverdrup still believed that all was well, and that in due time his leader would turn up safe and sound; but the spirits of the others went down to zero, and it was unanimously agreed to go home to Norway, to see if any news had been received, and if not, as the *Fram* was still amply supplied with all things needful, at once to go in search of the two explorers.

On arriving at Skjærvö, Sverdrup at once made his way to the telegraph-office with a bundle of telegrams; but as the hour was somewhere about midnight, he was not very graciously received, until he mentioned who he was and whence he came. The manager's tone then changed as if by magic: nothing was too good for Sverdrup and the *Fram*, and in an astonishingly short space of time the official jumped into his clothes, and came to the door with the welcome words on his lips, "Nansen and Johansen have come back."

Sverdrup waited to hear no more; he rushed off to tell his comrades, and in a few minutes the guns of the *Fram* gave voice to her salute to the great deed her master had accomplished. But there was much to be done: the whole world was waiting for the news of the *Fram's* return, and soon the telegraph clerks were ticking off message after message as fast as their fingers could move. One of the first messages was, of course, sent to Nansen, who was then at Hammerfest: "*Fram* arrived safely; all well on board; leaves at once for Tromsö. Welcome home."

The welcome dispatch reached him early in the morning, and that same day he and Fru Nansen, who had arrived the evening before, sailed for Tromsö. But the very best that steam could do seemed far too slow to Nansen just then, and his greeting flashed over the wires far in advance of him: "A thousand times welcome to you and all. Hurrah for the *Fram!*"

THE END.

www.ingramcontent.com/pod-product-compliance
Lightning Source LLC
Chambersburg PA
CBHW031252230426
43670CB00005B/148